TIMETABLES OF SPORTS HISTORY:
FOOTBALL

BY
William S. Jarrett

Facts On File
New York • Oxford

TIMETABLES OF SPORTS HISTORY: FOOTBALL

Facts On File, Inc.		Facts On File Limited
460 Park Avenue South	or	Collins Street
New York, New York 10016		Oxford OX4 1XJ
		United Kingdom

Library of Congress Cataloging-in-Publication Data

Jarrett, William.
  Timetables of sports history. Football / edited and compiled by William Jarrett.
    p. cm.
  Bibliography: p.
  Includes index.
  Summary: A chronological survey of college and professional football from the mid-nineteenth century to the present day.
  ISBN 0-8160-1919-3 (alk. paper)
  1. Football—United States—History—Chronology—Juvenile literature. [1. Football—History—Chronology.]   I. Title.
GV950.J37   1989
796.332'64—dc19   89-30418

British CIP data available upon request

Facts On File books are available at special discounts when purchased in bulk quantities for businesses, associations, institutions, or sales promotion. Please contact the Special Sales Department at 212/683-2244. (Dial 1-800-322-8755, except in NY, AK, HI)

Text & Jacket Design by Ron Monteleone
Composition by Facts On File, Inc.
Printed in the United States of America

10 9 8 7 6 5 4 3 2 1

This book is printed on acid-free paper.

CONTENTS

PREFACE

American football, as we know it today, began more than 125 years ago on the playing fields of the nation's elite colleges and universities—Yale, Princeton and Harvard, to name a few—and spread quickly to the four corners of the continent. It was a game devised by and for privileged amateur athletes in search of a rugged sport they could call their own, and it grew into a national pastime dominated by young men drawn largely from working-class America, many of whom are now paid millions to display their talents. In the beginning, perhaps a handful of spectators turned out to watch young footballers throw themselves at each other with such reckless abandon. Now tens of millions view these modern-day gladiators from the comfort of their living rooms.

Football in the late 19th century was a far cry from the game we know today. When Princeton played Rutgers on November 6, 1869, in what is generally regarded as the first game of intercollegiate football, the few who watched it saw a form of soccer, with 25 men on a side. It was illegal to run with the ball or to pass it, and only the influence of Harvard, where a combination of rugby and soccer prevailed, saved the day for the sport that evolved into American football.

Here's how it happened. Harvard's arch rival, Yale, played soccer-style football only, and it wasn't until 1875 that the two schools were able to reach a compromise on playing a game that was part rugby and part soccer. Harvard won that first game, 4 to 0, and the two schools have been playing football against each other ever since. Soon every major school in the country—including Army, Navy, Notre Dame, Stanford, Michigan and Alabama—was playing the game, which became so rough that in 1906 President Theodore Roosevelt almost banned the sport.

Professional football wasn't far behind. Pudge Heffelfinger, Yale's great All-American, was reputedly the first player to accept payment for playing football. That happened in 1892. Soon semi-professional teams throughout Ohio and Pennsylvania were forming loosely constructed leagues and playing each other for fun and profit as well. It wasn't until 1920, though, that the forerunner of the National Football League (NFL)—called the American Professional Football Association—was organized, with 10 midwestern teams participating and the immortal Jim Thorpe serving as its first president. The rest is history, and that's what this book is all about: a year-by-year account of the game of football.

If, as nonfollowers of the sport frequently insist, football is "only a game," then why does it create such autumn madness throughout America? Perhaps the answer lies in the following quote from a 1949 report published by Rutgers University, where the game began 80 years earlier: "If Wellington was right that the Battle of Waterloo was won on the playing fields of Eton, then it's a good bet that the battles of the Marne, Chateau-Thierry, Guadalcanal and Anzio were won on playing fields that trace their histories back to some goings on in New Brunswick [NJ] on an afternoon 80 long years ago."

We are indebted to Yale Library for rare photos of the early days in college football, and to the National Collegiate Athletic Association (NCAA) for its help and cooperation. On the professional side, we wish to thank Malcolm Emmons and NFL Properties for their help in providing the many fine photographs of NFL stars scattered throughout the book. Thanks also to Terri Stramiello for her help in researching the thousands of facts that went into the production of this unique work.

HOW TO USE THIS BOOK

In Football Timetables, you will find the colorful history of the game arranged in chronological order, with each page (from 1920 on) comprised of three separate columns representing one year. The first two columns record the major events and highlights for that year in college and professional football, respectively, during the regular season. Here you'll find the names of the leading players and their records. Under the "College" column, you'll also find the National Collegiate Athletic Association's consensus All-American team for that year, along with the major college conference champions and the Heisman Trophy winners. The "Professional" column lists the winners of each division in the National Football League, including the men who sparked their teams to victory.

The third column covers all postseason action, featuring major College Bowl results and the professional playoffs and championship games—and, from 1967 on, the Super Bowl results. All are described in some detail, including the leading scorers and the most significant plays. In the 1940 championship game, for example, the Chicago Bears trounced Washington, 73 to 0, the worst defeat in NFL history. And yet, only three weeks earlier, Washington had defeated Chicago in a regular season game, holding the Bears to only 3 points. Quarterback Sid Luckman starred for the Bears in their rout of the Redskins, while the defense held Washington to only 55 yards on the ground and intercepted 8 passes thrown by Sammy Baugh, pro football's leading passer at the time. Readers should bear in mind that most of the post season activity, both college and professional, includes games played in the calendar year following the regular season. Thus, Super Bowl I, which actually took place in January 1967, is included in the 1966 coverage. The same applies to the college bowl games, many of which are played on New Years Day.

You'll probably notice a few instances where a player's first name isn't given. This is not an oversight, but the result of unavailable information. In the early days of football, sports journalism was primitive and inconsistent, and most sources used first names only sporadically.

If you're looking for a particular player, but you don't know what year(s) he played, check the index in the back of the book. Using the above example, you'll find references to both Luckman and Baugh, along with other Bear and Redskin standouts such as Joe Maniaci, Bill Osmanski, Bulldog Turner and Andy Farkas.

Abbreviations for positions are as follows: B: Back, C: Center, DB: Defensive Back, E: End, G: Guard, K: Kicker, P: Punter, PK: Place Kicker, L: Lineman, LB: Linebacker, OB: Offensive Back, T: Tackle, TE: Tight End, WR: Wide Receiver.

COLLEGE
1865-1875

1869: The first intercollegiate football game in the U.S. takes place in New Brunswick, N.J., between Princeton and Rutgers. Each goal—or touchdown, as it is later called—counts one point, and the first team to score 6 goals is declared the winner. Rutgers wins, 6-4.

1872: Yale organizes a football team, using soccer rules to a large degree, and beats Columbia, 3-0, in its first and only game of that year.

1873: Yale invites Harvard (which declines), Princeton, Columbia and Rutgers to a meeting in N.Y. to draft a set of rules. They call themselves the Intercollegiate Football Association. Some of the rules they agree on are: Players may not run with the ball…Only lateral or backward passes are allowed…Tackling below the waist is illegal…Field size is 140 yds long and 70 yds wide…Game is divided into two 45-minute halves. In the first game played under the new rules, Princeton defeats Yale, 3-0, at New Haven, Ct.

1874: Harvard plays McGill University (Montreal, Canada) three times using modified rugby rules. Running with the ball (which is now oblong instead of round) is permitted. The "extra point" following each TD is introduced.

1875: Yale and Harvard meet for the first time using mostly rugby rules. Harvard wins, 4 goals to 0.

COLLEGE
1875-1885

1877: Teams now consist of 15 players. with 9 men on line, a quarterback, 2 halfbacks, a three-quarter back and 2 fullbacks.

1879: American-style football spreads westward. The University of Michigan and an amateur team from Racine, Wis., meet for the first time on a baseball field in Chicago. Michigan wins by a TD and goal.

1880: Walter Camp, an all-round athlete at Yale, leads the fight to establish new rules for American football. Teams are reduced to 11 men, including 7 linemen, a quarterback, 2 halfbacks and a fullback. The quarterback stands behind the center, takes the snap and hands off to a back. The field is reduced in size to 110 yds long and 53 yds wide.

1882: The modern concept of "downs" and "yards to gain" is introduced, along with signal-calling.

1883: Walter Camp advocates a new scoring system: 5 points for a field goal, 4 points for a free kick after a TD, 2 points for a TD and 1 point for a safety.

The wedge formation is introduced by Princton in a game against Pennsylvania. It allows blockers to form a V-shaped wedge in front of the ball carrier, providing interference and allowing him to advance the ball. A TD is now worth 4 points and the conversion is 2 points.

COLLEGE
1885-1890

1886: John W. Heisman plays football for the first time with his high-school team in western Pa.

1887: Pennsylvania plays Rutgers in the first indoor football game at Madison Square Garden, N.Y. Notre Dame plays its first intercollegiate game, losing to Michigan, 8-0 (Nov. 23).

1888: The offensive line now sets up in close formation, shoulder to shoulder. Backs also close ranks to facilitate use of the T-formation. Walter Camp is Yale's first head coach. His team wins all 14 games without giving up a point and scores 704 points itself. Outstanding players for Yale include Amos Alonzo Stagg, Pudge Heffelfinger, Kid Wallace, Charlie Gill, Pa Corbin, George Woodruff, Billy Bull, Lee McClung, Capt. "Pot" Graves and Bill Wurtemberg.

1889: Walter Camp announces his first All-American team (published in *The Week's Sport*, a N.Y. periodical):

E: Amos Alonzo Stagg (Yale), Arthur Cumnock (Harvard)
T: Hector Cowan (Princeton), Charles Gill (Yale)
G: W.W. "Pudge" Heffelfinger (Yale), Jesse Riggs (Princeton)
C: William George (Princeton)
B: Edgar Allan Poe* (Princeton), Roscoe Channing (Princeton), Knowlton Ames (Princeton), James Lee (Harvard)
*Poe is a grandnephew of the famous American writer.

1890: The first Army-Navy game is played on Nov. 29 on the Parade Ground at West Point. The idea is pushed by Cadet Dennis Michie (after whom the present Army stadium is named). Navy wins, 24-0.

COLLEGE
1890-1900

1892: Harvard introduces the "flying wedge," a modification of Princeton's wedge formation. Harvard's offensive linemen and 2 backs form 2 lanes about 20 yds downfield from the ball. Starting in unison, they run at full speed to the ball. When the back picks it up, the mass momentum of his blockers creates an impenetrable wall of interference. The Rules Committee later makes all wedge formations illegal.

Amos Alonzo Stagg, former Yale Star and All-American, becomes the first head football coach at the University of Chicago. He remains in that position 41 years, producing several championship teams (see also *1905*, et al, and *Stagg* bio).

1894: Harvard, Pennsylvania, Princeton and Yale form a new Rules Committee. It reduces the length of the game from 90 minutes to 70 minutes (two 35-minute halves) and makes it illegal for more than 3 offensive men to move before the ball is put into play.

George Woodruff, head coach at Pennsylvania, introduces the "guards back" formation. His teams dominate eastern football for the next few seasons.

1895: Chicago, Illinois, Michigan, Minnesota, Northwestern, Purdue and Wisconsin organize a new football conference (the future Big Ten).

1897: The scoring system is revised. TD = 5 points; conversion = 1; field goal = 5; safety = 2.

1899: Glenn "Pop" Warner is named head coach at Carlisle (Pa.) Indian School, where he develops the famous single- and double-wing formations. In Warner's first year, his team beats eastern powers Pennsylvania, Columbia, plus the University of California.

AMOS ALONZO STAGG
(1862-1965)

Known affectionately during his coaching years as the "Grand Old Man of Football," Stagg learned how to play the game at Yale, where he starred at end and was named to Walter Camp's first All-American team (see *1889*). He was also the ace pitcher on Yale's baseball team, which won 5 championships during his era.

In 1892, Stagg was named head coach at the University of Chicago, the first to be given faculty status (he was later made a full professor, another first). Five of Stagg's Chicago teams went undefeated, and 12 others lost only one game. His most famous team was the 1905 squad, which went undefeated in 9 games and starred Walter Eckersall at quarterback.

Stagg remained head coach at Chicago for 40 years, retiring in 1932. He then headed west and coached at the College (now University) of the Pacific for another 14 years, retiring at the age of 85. Still feeling too young to quit, he helped his son coach at Susquehanna University (Selinsgrove, Pa.) for 5 more years, leaving in 1953 to take care of his ailing wife.

In 1943, Stagg was voted Coach of the Year by his fellow coaches and football's Man of the Year by America's sports writers. In 1951 he was among the first men elected to the National Football Hall of Fame (and is the only one elected as both player and coach).

COLLEGE
1900-1905

1901: Michigan, coached by Fielding "Hurry-Up" Yost, ends its season undefeated (12-0) and is invited to the first "Rose Bowl" game to be played in Pasadena (Calif.) on New Year's Day (1902). The first of Yost's famous "point-a-minute" teams, Michigan crushes Stanford (3-1-2), 49-0. Game is called when the Stanford captain informs Michigan, "If you are willing, we are ready to call it quits."

1902: Amos Alonzo Stagg, head coach at the University of Chicago, is the first to use a backfield shift.

1903: Carlisle Indians' coach Glenn "Pop" Warner introduces the hidden-ball trick against Harvard to score the winning TD (see also *1899*).

1903: A new 30,000-seat stadium, the first ever designed especially for football, is completed at Harvard.

Princeton wins the national college football championship with 11-0 record.

1904: The last of the University of Michigan's "point-a-minute" teams (1901-1904) plays its final game. Under coach Yost (see *1902*), they are undefeated in 4 years, with only a tie to mar an otherwise perfect record. A total of 6 TDs are scored against Michigan during that period, with 4 of them the result of fumbles. Michigan's offense, meanwhile, runs up 2,821 points. Coach Yost himself, however, rates his 1925 Michigan team, featuring Bernie Oosterbaan, as his best squad.

Pennsylvania is named national college football champion (12 wins, no losses).

COLLEGE
1905-1910

1905: After 11 players die and 104 others are seriously injured in college football during 1905, President Theodore Roosevelt issues an order that rough play must be eliminated or he will abolish the game. The Rules Committee under Walter Camp (see *Camp* bio) quickly takes steps, legalizing the forward pass (to open up the game) and adopting other rule changes that "debrutalize" college football.

Chicago ends Michigan's 56-game unbeaten streak, 2-0, in the final game of the season at Marshall Field (now Stagg Field) in Chicago. The largest crowd in football history (25,791) attends. Played under "old" rules, forward passing is not allowed, and only 5 yds are needed (in 3 downs) to make a 1st down. The game is won on a safety in the closing minutes.

1906: St. Louis University, coached by Eddie Cochens, is the first team to experiment with the forward pass following the rule change. Wesleyan (Ct.) is also among the first to use the forward pass in its game against Yale, when Sammy Moore throws to Irvin Van Tassell for 18 yds.

1907: Yale is named national college football champion, winning all 9 games on its schedule.

The Carlisle Indians, coached by Pop Warner, enjoy a near-perfect season, defeating Pennsylvania, Minnesota, Harvard and Chicago. Their only loss is to Princeton. The starting lineup includes Little Old Man, Afraid of Bear, Lubo the Wolf and Mount Pleasant. Jim Thorpe, a freshman, makes his first appearance.

1908: The University of Chicago uses the "Statue of Liberty" play for the first time.

Washington & Jefferson (Pa.) is the first college team to put numbers on its players' uniforms (an idea that comes from track and field).

1909: The point value of a field goal drops to 3, as it remains today.

WALTER CAMP
(1859-1925)

As a freshman at Yale, Walter Camp played in the first Yale-Harvard rugby game in 1876, the same year the Intercollegiate Football Association (Harvard, Yale, Princeton, Columbia and Rutgers) was formed. From then on, Camp led the fight to transform soccer and rugby into what we now know as American football. He sponsored the concept of scrimmage lines (replacing rugby's "scrum") and installed the system of downs and yards to gain (first 5, then 10). He also fought for 11 men on a side (instead of rugby's 15) with 7 men on the line and 4 in the backfield.

In 1883, Camp proposed a new point-scoring system, which led eventually to the modern system, and 3 years later he established (through the Collegiate Rules Committee) a neutral zone along the scrimmage line. In 1888, he advocated tackling below the waist and changing the blocking rules, which indirectly brought about the T-formation, with the quarterback standing behind the center.

Camp's most important contribution to the game came in 1906, when as head of the American Collegiate Football Rules Committee, forerunner of the NCAA (National Collegiate Athletic Association), he saved football from extinction as the public reacted against excessive roughness and low scores. Legalization of the forward pass was critical in resolving the crisis.

At Yale, Camp was an all-round athlete who played halfback for 6 years and also starred in baseball, track, tennis, and water sports. He was Yale's first football coach (1888) and selected the first All-American team (1889), with Casper Whitney.

COLLEGE
1910-1915

1911: Led by Jim Thorpe, an All-American and future Olympics star, the Carlisle Indian School (see also *1907*) defeats nationally ranked Harvard, 18-15, in one of the greatest upsets in college football history.

1912: Carlisle routs Army, 35-13, behind the running and passing of Jim Thorpe. One of the Army cadets assigned to stop Thorpe is a young linebacker named Dwight D. Eisenhower.

1913: In their first meeting, Notre Dame upsets a nationally ranked Army team, 35-13, using its new passing offense, starring quarterback Gus Dorais and his favorite receivers, including Knute Rockne. Although the forward pass has been used for several years (see *1906*), it has never received the kind of attention that Notre Dame's win over Army provides. In the game, Dorais completes 14 out of 17 pass attempts for 243 yds.

1915-1920

COLLEGE
1915-1916

1915: In the 2d Tournament of Roses Association football game (later to become the Rose Bowl game), which is played on Jan. 1, 1916, Washington State defeats Brown, 14-0. Cornell (9-0- 0) is declared the national college football champion.

1916: Four Pacific Coast schools form a new football league, which evolves years later into the Pac-10. It includes the universities of California, Oregon, Oregon State and Washington.

Dave Tibbott of Princeton dropkicks the ball 46 yds (a new college record) in a game against Tufts.

The most lopsided score in football history is recorded when Georgia Tech, coached by John Heisman (after whom the now famous Heisman Trophy is named), beats Cumberland, 222-0. Georgia kicker Jim Preas boots 18 extra points in the first half alone.

Oregon defeats Pennsylvania, 14-0, in the 3d annual Rose Bowl game. Pittsburgh (8-0-0) is voted the #1 team in the nation.

COLLEGE
1917-1918

1917: Georgia Tech wins all its games by huge margins: 41-0 over Pennsylvania; 98-0 over Carlisle; 83-0 over Vanderbilt; 68- 7 over Auburn; 48-0 over Tulane; and 63-0 over Washington & Lee. Not surprisingly, Georgia Tech (9-0-0) is declared the national champion.

The Mare Island Marines beat the Camp Lewis Army team, 19-7, in the annual Rose Bowl game as World War I sends most able-bodied men into the armed services.

1918: The Great Lakes Naval Training Station defeats the Mare Island Marines, 17-0, in the Rose Bowl game. Pittsburgh (4- 1-0) is the nation's top-ranked team in a season cut short by wartime restrictions.

COLLEGE
1919

1919: Harvard edges out Oregon, 7-6, at the 6th annual Rose Bowl game. It is the only postseason game played in Harvard's football history. The Cantabs, with a record of 9-0-1, are named the #1 team in the nation.

The following All-American team, selected by the Football Writers Association of America, represents the best college players during the period from 1869, when the first intercollegiate game was played, to 1920, when the post-WWI sports boom and the formation of the first professional football league changed the course of college football: Josh Cody (Vanderbilt), Walt Eckersall (Chicago), Huntington Hardwick (Harvard), Wilbur "Fats" Henry (Washington & Jefferson), Willie Heston (Michigan), Frank Hinkey (Yale), Elmer Oliphant (Army, Purdue), Truxton Hare (Pennsylvania), W.W. "Pudge" Heffelfinger (Princeton), Adolph "Germany" Schultz (Michigan), Jim Thorpe (Carlisle).

1890-1920

PROFESSIONAL 1890-1900

1892: Pudge Heffelfinger, three-time All-American from Yale, becomes the first known professional football player, accepting money to represent the Pittsburgh (Pa.) Allegheny Athletic Association in its game against the Pittsburgh Athletic Club. Heffelfinger scores a TD and receives $500 (under the table).

1894: The Greensburg (Pa.) Athletic Association hires ex-Princeton player, Lawson Fiscus, for $20 a game.

1895: Latrobe (Pa.) hires quarterback John Brallier for $10 a game plus expenses. Latrobe defeats Jeannette (Pa.), 12-0 (Aug. 31). Later that year, Duquesne Country & Athletic Club (DC & AC) makes $4,000 profit using college stars.

1896: The Allegheny Athletic Assocation hires Heffelfinger and other Ivy League players and defeats both Pittsburgh AC and DC & AC.

1897: Touchdown increases in value from 4 to 5 points. Point after touchdown (PAT) is reduced from 2 points to 1.

1898: Steel magnate William C. Temple buys out Pittsburgh's DC & AC team, which goes undefeated for 2 years.

PROFESSIONAL 1900-1910

1900: A.C. Dinkey, owner of Homestead Library & Athletic Club, lures Pittsburgh DC & AC players away with higher salaries.

1902: Philadelphia Athletics and Phillies baseball clubs organize pro football teams in Philadelphia and Pittsburgh, creating what they call the "National Football League." N.Y. Giant pitcher (and future Hall of Fame member) Christy Mathewson plays fullback for Pittsburgh.

The Philadelphia Athletics win the first night football game ever played, 39-0, against Kanaweola AC (Elmira, N.Y.).

1903: Massillon (Ohio) Tigers defeat Akron (Ohio) for the state championship using pros from the Pittsburgh team.

Charles Follis is the first black pro football player (Shelby AC).

1905: Canton (Ohio) Bulldogs are formed with Willie Heston, former University of Michigan All-American, in charge. The team loses the Ohio championship to Massillon in 1905.

1906: Several rule changes are made in pro football: The forward pass is legalized...A neutral zone along scrimmage line is established...Ten yds are required in 3 downs to make 1st down...And at least 6 players per team must be on the line of scrimmage before the ball is snapped.

PROFESSIONAL 1910-1920

1912: More rule changes: TDs now count for 6 points...The field is reduced in size to 100 yds...The number of downs allowed to make 10 yds is increased to 4.

1915: Toledo, Youngstown, Akron and Dayton join Massillon, Canton and Columbus in the Ohio League. Canton hires Jim Thorpe, former star at Carlisle Indian School (and Olympic decathlon champion in 1912). He leads the team to victory over arch rival Massillon, 4-0.

1916: Canton and Massillon play a scoreless tie before 10,000 fans, the largest turnout ever for pro football.

1917: World War I slows further development of pro football.

1919: George Halas signs a contract with Hammond (Ind.). Curly Lambeau organizes the Green Bay Packers in Wisconsin. The stage is set for the development of the American Professional Football Association (APFA). (See *1920*.)

Yale's undefeated championship team of 1888 (above) scores 698 points to its opponents' 0. Team members include All-Americans **Pudge Heffelfinger, Amos Alonzo Stagg, Charlie Gill, Pa Corbin, Kid Wallace** and **George Woodruff.**

Pudge Heffelfinger (left) and **Bum Mc-Clung,** both All-Americans at Yale in 1891.

Walter C. Camp, "Father of American Football."

Frank Hinkey, a four-time All-American end at Yale during the 1890s.

One of America's most famous athletes ever: **Jim Thorpe,** All-American from Carlisle Indian School.
Cumberland County Historical society, Carlisle, PA

An artist's rendering of the first intercollegiate football game between **Princeton** and **Rutgers** at New Brunswick, N.J. on Nov. 6, 1869.

1920

COLLEGE REGULAR SEASON

All-American George Gipp, backfield star at Notre Dame, dies of pneumonia only 3 weeks after leading his team to its 2d undefeated season in a row. Gipp's inspirational character is later portrayed by actor Ronald Reagan in a film about Notre Dame coach Knute Rockne.

University of California (9-0-0) wins the national college football championship (see also under *College Bowl Games*).

1920 All-American Team
E: Luke Urban (Boston College), Charles Carney (Illinois), Bill Fincher (Georgia Tech)
T: Stan Keck (Princeton), Ralph Scott (Wisconsin)
G: Tim Callahan (Yale), Tom Woods (Harvard), Iolas Huffman (Ohio State)
C: Herb Stein (Pittsburgh)
B: George Gipp (Notre Dame), Donald Lourie (Princeton), Gaylord Stinchcomb (Ohio State), Charles Way (Penn State)

PROFESSIONAL REGULAR SEASON

Ten teams form the American Professional Football Association (APFA): Decatur Staleys, Canton Bulldogs, Akron Pros, Dayton Triangles, Cleveland Tigers, Rock Island Independents, Chicago Cardinals, Hammond Pros, Muncie Flyers and Rochester Jeffersons. Jim Thorpe is named president of the new league.

Detroit Heralds, Chicago Tigers, Buffalo All-Americans and Columbus Panhandlers are included in APFA schedules but are not official league members.

Akron Pros are the best Ohio team, featuring black star wingback Fritz Pollard and tailback Rip King. The defense allows only 7 points in 9 games.

The top Illinois team is Decatur Staleys, followed by the Chicago Cardinals, who split a 2-game series with the Staleys. Chicago star Paddy Driscoll is paid $300 per game.

The Buffalo All-Americans, featuring Lou Little, Swede Youngstrom, Lud Wray and Ockie Anderson, are rated best in the East.

In a game between Canton and Buffalo on Dec. 4 at the Polo Grounds in New York, 15,000 fans watch superstar Jim Thorpe play for Canton. Buffalo wins the game, 7-3. The next day, Dec. 5, the Buffalo All-Americans host the Akron Pros in Buffalo and play to a scoreless tie. And a week later, Akron and Decatur also play a scoreless tie in Chicago. The Akron Pros (6-0-3) are then declared the first APFA champions.

COLLEGE BOWL GAMES

ROSE BOWL:
California 28, Ohio State 0
Brick Muller, California's All-Star American end, stars on offense and defense before 42,000 fans in Pasadena. His 50-yd pass to Ted Stephens is the longest ever completed in the Rose Bowl. California's passing attack outperforms the famous Ohio State aerial circus which led the Big Ten during the regular season. The Buckeye's All-American quarterback, Pete Stinchcomb, is under constant pressure from a strong California line led by Capt. Cort Majors.

1921

COLLEGE REGULAR SEASON

Little Centre College (Danville, Ky.) travels to Cambridge (Mass.) to face mighty Harvard, unbeaten in its last 25 games (including a victory over Oregon in the 1920 Rose Bowl). Centre upsets the Crimson, 6-0, when quarterback Bo McMillin breaks loose for a 32-yd TD run in the 3d quarter.

Following their upset win over Harvard, Centre College's "Praying Colonels" are themselves upset by Texas A&M, 22-14, in Dallas, Texas. The Texans, 20-point underdogs, score a safety early in the first quarter. Centre moves ahead early in the 3d quarter, 7-2, but A&M scores 20 unanswered points to win handily. Bo McMillin, Centre's All-American quarterback, who marries his high-school sweetheart the day before the game, is intercepted in the 4th quarter, leading to the final Texas TD.

Cornell, with a record of 8 wins and no losses, is named the top college football team in the nation.

1921 All-American Team
E: Brick Muller (California), Eddie Anderson (Notre Dame)
T: Dan McMillan (California), Iolas Huffman (Ohio State)
G: Frank Schwab (Lafayette), John Brown (Harvard), Stan Keck (Princeton)
C: Herb Stein (Pittsburgh)
B: Aubrey Devine (Iowa), Glenn Killinger (Penn State), Bo McMillin (Centre), Malcolm Aldrich (Yale), Edgar Kaw (Cornell)

PROFESSIONAL REGULAR SEASON

Joe Carr replaces Jim Thorpe as APFA president.

League membership expands to 21. New teams include Green Bay, Minneapolis, Cincinnati, Evansville, Louisville, Tonawanda, Washington and New York. The only non-returnee is the Chicago Tigers. The Staleys move from Decatur to Chicago.

Paul Robeson, former All-American at Rutgers, later to become a world-famous singer, actor and political activist, signs a contract with the Akron Pros.

The Columbus Panhandlers include five Nesser brothers. A sixth brother is top lineman for Akron.

Jimmy Conzelman is named player-coach of the Rock Island Independents.

Jim Thorpe signs with the Cleveland Tigers but suffers broken ribs in a game against Cincinnati and is out for the season.

Undefeated Buffalo and Chicago Staleys meet in Wrigley Field (Chicago). Buffalo wins, 7-6. Later, Buffalo beats Akron, 14-0, in Akron, then travels all night to Chicago and loses its first game the next day in a rematch with the Chicago Staleys, 10-7. The Staleys are then named APFA champions at the annual league meeting.

APFA All-Stars include Curly Lambeau and Cub Buck (Green Bay), Rip King and Fritz Pollard (Akron), Swede Youngstrom (Canton), Jimmy Conzelman (Rock Island), Paddy Driscoll (Chicago Cardinals), Lou Little, Lud Wray and Tommy Hughitt (Buffalo), and George Halas and Dutch Sternaman (Chicago Staleys).

COLLEGE BOWL GAMES

ROSE BOWL:
   California 0, Washington & Jefferson 0
California, heavily favored to win, is outplayed by undefeated Washington & Jefferson and barely manages to salvage a scoreless tie. An offside penalty costs the Presidents from Pennsylvania the victory after halfback Wayne Brenkert breaks through the right side of the California line. Two field goal attempts by W & J late in the game also fail to register. California manages only 2 first downs and is forced to kick on first down throughout much of the game. W & J plays the entire game without making a substitution. California's All-American end and passer, Brick Muller, fails to complete a pass for the first time all season.

COLLEGE REGULAR SEASON

Illinois (8-0-0), coached by Bob Zuppke, is named national college football champion. Princeton is rated the best team in the East, with Cornell second and Army third. All 3 teams end the season undefeated (but Army plays 2 tie games, against Yale and Notre Dame).

In Philadelphia, Army beats Navy, 17-14, for the first time since WWI.

Princeton's undefeated "Team of Destiny," coached by Bill Roper, plays its first game in the midwest (and final game of the season) against the University of Chicago. Behind 18-7 in the 4th quarter, the Tigers rally to win, 21-18, in what losing coach Amos Alonzo Stagg of Chicago calls the greatest game he has ever seen.

Iowa and Michigan tie for the lead in the Western Conference. Chicago is also undefeated in the conference but has 1 tie.

California is named top team on the Pacific Coast. Nebraska is champion of the Missouri Valley. Vanderbilt and Georgia Tech are strongest in the South.

1922 All-American Team
E: W.H. Taylor (Navy), Harold Muller (California)
T: C. Herbert Treat (Princeton), John Thurman (Pennsylvania)
G: Frank Schwab (Lafayette), Charles Hubbard (Harvard)
C: Ed Garbisch (Army)
B: Gordon Locke (Iowa), Edgar Law (Cornell), Harry Kipke (Michigan), John Thomas (Chicago)

PROFESSIONAL REGULAR SEASON

George Halas takes control of the Staleys and changes the name of this Chicago franchise to Bears. He also leads the way in renaming APFA: It is now the National Football League (NFL).

The Toledo Maroons, Milwaukee Badgers, Racine Legion and Oorang (Marion, Ohio) Indians (led by Jim Thorpe) are added to the league; 7 others are dropped when they fail to raise $1,000 forfeit fees.

Wilbur "Fats" Henry, Canton tackle, drop-kicks a 50-yd field goal against Toledo, the longest ever.

The Canton Bulldogs are reorganized under Guy Chamberlin. After blanking the Akron Pros, 22-0, and beating the Chicago Cardinals 7-6, the Bulldogs go on to win the NFL championship with a 10-0-2 record.

Jimmy Conzelman (Milwaukee Badgers player-coach) runs for a record 5 TDs against Rock Island (Oct. 15). He leads the NFL in rushing and passing TDs for the season.

The Green Bay Packers, now insolvent, become a public nonprofit corporation. Green Bay residents can buy shares at $5 each.

NFL All-Star team includes Guy Chamberlin (Canton), Luke Urban (Buffalo), Hugh Blacklock (Chicago Bears), Tommy Hughitt (Buffalo), Paddy Driscoll (Chicago Cardinals) and Rip King (Akron).

COLLEGE BOWL GAMES

ROSE BOWL:
USC 14, Penn State 3
Before a record crowd of 53,000 in Pasadena's Rose Bowl, the University of Southern California defeats Penn State, 14-3. The start of the game is delayed 35 minutes because the cars carrying the Penn State team to the stadium are unable to make their way through the Tournament of Roses traffic, causing the game to end in semi-darkness. Penn State goes ahead on a field goal in the first period, but the Trojans connect with TDs in the 2d and 3d quarters while holding the vaunted Penn State offense in check the rest of the way.

COLLEGE REGULAR SEASON

Yale, led by coach Tad Jones, produces the best team in the East, beating arch rivals Princeton and Harvard on successive Saturdays.

Illinois and Michigan tie for the lead in the Western Conference. Nebraska and Kansas are best in the Missouri Valley, while California and Washington share honors on the Pacific Coast.

1923 All-American Team

E: Lynn Bomar (Vanderbilt), Homer Hazel (Rutgers)
T: Century Milstead (Yale), Frank Sundstrom (Cornell)
G: Charles Hubbard (Harvard), Jack Blott (Michigan)
C: Joe Bedenk (Penn State)
B: George Pfann (Cornell), Red Grange (Illinois), Earl Martineau (Minnesota), Bill Mallory (Yale)

PROFESSIONAL REGULAR SEASON

Evansville is the only team dropped from the NFL in 1923. New franchises in Duluth, St. Louis and Cleveland are added.

Lou Smyth (Canton Bulldogs) leads the NFL in rushing and passing TDs. He and Jimmy Conzelman are the only players in NFL history to do this.

Wilbur "Fats" Henry of Canton punts the ball 94 yds in a game against Akron to set still another record (see *1922*).

Canton wins its 2d straight undefeated NFL championship. A key game against the Chicago Bears ends in a 6-0 win for the Bulldogs.

Paddy Driscoll (Chicago Cardinals) leads the NFL in scoring with 78 points, including 10 field goals.

George Halas of the Chicago Bears picks up a fumble by Jim Thorpe (Oorang Indians) and races 98 yds for a TD, a new NFL record.

NFL All-Star Team

E: Inky Williams (Hammond), Gus Tebell (Columbus)
T: Ed Healey (Chicago Bears), Pete Henry (Canton)
G: Swede Youngstrom (Buffalo), Bub Weller (St. Louis)
C: Harry Mehre (Minneapolis)
B: Paddy Driscoll (Chicago Cardinals), Jim Thorpe (Oorang), Al Michaels (Akron), Doc Elliot (Canton)

COLLEGE BOWL GAMES

ROSE BOWL:
Washington 14, Navy 14
Navy's powerful passing attack (16 completions) is offset by Washington's courageous goal-line stands. Navy scores first on a 17-yd pass from quarterback McKee to halfback Cullen in the 2d quarter. A TD pass from fullback Shapley to McKee lifts Navy to a 14-0 lead. Washington cuts the lead to 14-7 before the first half ends on a spectacular 23-yd run by halfback Wilson. The only score in the 2d half comes on a recovered fumble on Navy's 10-yd line, followed by a short pass from Washington quarterback Abel to Bryan. A last-minute field goal attempt by Washington from Navy's 22-yd line sails off to the left.

COLLEGE REGULAR SEASON

In a game against Michigan, Red Grange, the "Galloping Ghost" of Illinois, returns the opening kickoff 95 yds for a TD, scores 3 more TDs on consecutive runs of 67, 56 and 45 yds, all within 12 minutes, and then passes for a 5th TD.

At the Polo Grounds in New York before 55,000 fans, Notre Dame defeats Army, 13-7. The Fighting Irish backfield of Don Miller, Elmer Layden, Jim Crowley and Harry Stuhldreyer, known as "The Four Horsemen," lead the way.

Yale, Dartmouth and Pennsylvania dominate the East. All are undefeated (but tied).

Chicago, undefeated but tied 3 times, wins the Western Conference. Stanford and California are best in the Far West. Alabama and Centre lead the South.

1924 All-American Team

E: H.B. Bjorkman (Dartmouth), Charles Berry (Lafayette)
T: Ed McGinley (Pennsylvania), Ed Weir (Nebraska)
G: Edliff Slaughter (Michigan), E.C. Horrell (California)
C: Ed Garbisch (Army)
B: Harry Stuhldreyer (Notre Dame), Red Grange (Illinois), Walter Koppisch (Columbia), Homer Hazel (Rutgers)

PROFESSIONAL REGULAR SEASON

Frankford (Pa.) Yellowjackets and Kansas City Blues are added to the NFL. The Toledo franchise moves to Kenosha (Wis.). St. Louis, Louisville, Oorang (Marion, Ohio) and Toledo franchises are dropped.

Two-time NFL champion Canton Bulldogs are sold. The team moves to Cleveland for the 1924 season with Guy Chamberlin as coach.

The Frankford Yellowjackets become the first East Coast team, featuring eastern college stars, including Tex Hamer of Pennsylvania who rushes for 12 TDs. Frankford defeats the Cleveland Bulldogs, 12-7 (first defeat ever for a Guy Chamberlin-coached team).

Paddy Driscoll (Chicago Cardinals) drop-kicks a 50-yd field goal to tie Wilbur Henry's 1922 record.

The Chicago Bears beat the Cleveland Bulldogs in a postseason game and then claim the NFL championship. The league rules that the game does not count in the standings and awards the championship to Cleveland.

Curly Lambeau (Green Bay) is the first player to gain over 1,000 yds passing in one season.

NFL All-Star Team:

E: Joe Little Twig (Rock Island), Tillie Voss (Green Bay)
T: Ed Healey (Chicago Bears), Boni Petcoff (Columbus)
G: Swede Youngstrom (Buffalo), Stan Muirhead (Dayton)
C: George Trafton (Chicago Bears)
B: Joey Sternaman (Chicago Bears), Charlie Way (Frankford, Pa.), Benny Boynton (Buffalo), Doc Elliott (Cleveland)

COLLEGE BOWL GAMES

ROSE BOWL:
   Notre Dame 27, Stanford 10
In its first appearance in the Rose Bowl, Notre Dame wins in a battle of undefeated teams. The game marks the end of the "Four Horsemen," Notre Dame's legendary backfield. Fullback Ernie Nevers, Stanford's star, is slowed down by ankle injuries but still scores 2 TDs on runbacks of pass interceptions.

COLLEGE REGULAR SEASON

Coach Fielding Yost's Michigan team goes undefeated without allowing a point scored against it until the final game of the season, then loses to Northwestern, 3-2. Played in Soldier Field, Chicago, in poor weather, only 1 first down is made and 1 forward pass attempted in the entire game.

Walter Camp, "Father of American Football," dies in his sleep in a New York hotel room while attending a college football rules convention.

Undefeated Dartmouth, ranked #1 in the East, outscores its opponents, 340 to 29.

Alabama and Tulane dominate the South, and Washington is best in the far West.

Army tops Navy, 10-3, at sold-out Polo Grounds in New York.

1925 All-American Team

As selected by Grantland Rice and published in *Colliers* magazine from 1925 to 1947.

E: Bennie Oosterbaan (Michigan), George Tully (Dartmouth)
T: Ed Weir (Nebraska), Ralph Chase (Pittsburgh)
G: Carl Diehl (Dartmouth), Ed Hess (Ohio State)
C: Ed McMillan (Princeton)
B: Red Grange (Illinois), Andy Oberlander (Dartmouth), George Wilson (Washington), Ernie Nevers (Stanford)

PROFESSIONAL REGULAR SEASON

The Canton Bulldogs rejoin the NFL. The Providence Steam Roller, Detroit Panthers and Pottsville Maroons enter the league. Racine, Kenosha and Minneapolis drop out. Tim Mara buys the New York franchise for $500 and names his team the Giants.

Red Grange, All-American at the University of Illinois, quits school and joins the Chicago Bears. He makes his first appearance against the Chicago Cardinals on Thanksgiving Day and gains only 40 yds rushing. During an 18-game special tour to promote Grange, a record crowd of 73,000 watches Chicago play the N.Y. Giants at the Polo Grounds. The Bears win, 19-7, as Grange intercepts a pass and runs in for a TD. In all, Grange makes $50,000 during the tour.

Charlie Berry (Pottsville Maroons) leads the NFL in scoring (74 points). He later becomes a major league baseball catcher and longtime American League umpire.

The Pottsville Maroons, while in first place, are suspended by the league for playing an illegal exhibition game. The Chicago Cardinals capture the NFL title with an 11-2-1 record.

NFL All-Star Team

E: Charlie Berry (Pottsville), Ed Lynch (Rochester)
T: Ed Healey (Chicago Bears), Gus Sonnenberg (Detroit)
G: Art Carney (N.Y. Giants), Jim McMillin (Chicago Bears)
C: Ralph Claypool (Chicago Cardinals)
B: Joey Sternaman (Chicago Bears), Paddy Driscoll (Chicago Cardinals), Dave Noble (Cleveland), Jack McBride (N.Y. Giants)

COLLEGE BOWL GAMES

ROSE BOWL:
Alabama 20, Washington 19
This is the first appearance of a team from the deep South in the Rose Bowl. Alabama, coached by Wallace Wade, remains undefeated. Future film star Johnny Mack Brown is the Crimson Tide's outstanding player.

In the first East-West Shrine game, played at San Francisco, the College All-Stars from the West defeat the East All- Stars, 6-0.

1926

COLLEGE REGULAR SEASON

Notre Dame, undefeated and with only 7 points scored against it, is upset by Carnegie Tech, 19-0.

The Army-Navy game at Soldier's Field in Chicago draws 110,000 fans, the first college football game played before 100,000 or more. Game ends in a tie, 21-21.

Lafayette, Stanford (Pacific Coast Conference champ) and Alabama (Southern Conference leader) are the only major college teams to end the season undefeated.

Other Regional & Conference Leaders
EAST: Navy, Brown and Army
MISSOURI VALLEY: Oklahoma (Agricultural College)
ROCKY MOUNTAIN: Utah
SOUTHWESTERN: Southern Methodist

1926 All-American Team
E: Bennie Oosterbaan (Michigan), Vic Hanson (Syracuse)
T: Bud Sprague (Army), Frank Wickhorst (Navy)
G: Bernie Shively (Illinois), Harry Connaughton (Georgetown)
C: Bud Boeringer (Notre Dame)
B: Benny Friedman (Michigan), Mort Kaer (USC), Ralph Baker (Northwestern), Herb Joesting (Minnesota)

PROFESSIONAL REGULAR SEASON

C.C. Pyle (Red Grange's agent) forms the new American Football League, including Pyle's own team (N.Y. Yankees), plus Philadelphia, Newark (N.J.), Brooklyn, Boston, Chicago, Cleveland and Rock Island Independents (who jump from the NFL). The AFL loses money from the start and collapses at the end of the season.

In the NFL, the Pottsville Maroons (10-2-2) record 11 shutouts but finish 3d behind the Frankford (Pa.) Yellowjackets (14-1-2) and the Chicago Bears (14-1-2).

The Duluth Eskimos sign Ernie Nevers, All-American fullback from Stanford. He ranks 2d in scoring in his rookie year (71 points) and makes 7 interceptions on defense. Paddy Driscoll (Chicago Bears) is the top scorer in the NFL (86 points).

NFL All-Star Team
E: Brick Muller (Los Angeles), Charlie Berry (Pottsville)
T: Ed Healey (Chicago Bears), Walt Ellis (Chicago Cardinals)
G: Gus Sonnenberg (Detroit), Johnny Budd (Frankford, Pa.)
C: Clyde Smith (Kansas City)
B: Tut Imlay (Los Angeles), Paddy Driscoll (Chicago Bears), Verne Lewellen (Green Bay), Ernie Nevers (Duluth)

COLLEGE BOWL GAMES

ROSE BOWL:
  Alabama 7, Stanford 7
With 2 minutes to play, Alabama blocks a kick and scores the tying TD on a short burst up the middle by halfback Johnson. Caldwell's extra point try is good to give the Crimson Tide a tie before a capacity crowd of 60,000. Stanford scores its only TD in the 1st quarter on a 21-yd pass play from quarterback George Bogue to his end, Walker. Bogue then kicks the all-important extra point. Warm weather handicaps both teams, causing wholesale substitutions and several fumbles.

1927

COLLEGE REGULAR SEASON

The Rules Committee decides to set the goal posts 10 yds behind the goal line; it also sets time limits on the huddle and on putting the ball into play.

Notre Dame defeats Navy, 19-6, at Soldier Field, Chicago, before a record-breaking football crowd (114,000).

Georgia Tech is the top team in the South, while Yale and Dartmouth share honors in the East. Pittsburgh wins all its games (but is tied by Washington & Jefferson) to lead the Allegheny Mountain region.

Other Conference Champions
WESTERN: Illinois
SOUTHWESTERN: Texas A&M
PACIFIC COAST: Stanford & USC
ROCKY MOUNTAINS: Colorado A&M

1927 All-American Team
E: Bennie Oosterbaan (Michigan), Tom Nash (Georgia)
T: Jesse Hibbs (USC), Ed Hake (Pennsylvania)
G: John Smith (Notre Dame), Bill Webster (Yale)
C: John Charlesworth (Yale)
B: Morley Drury (USC), Red Cagle (Army), Gibby Welch (Pittsburgh), Herb Joesting (Minnesota)

PROFESSIONAL REGULAR SEASON

The NFL pares down its franchises from 22 to 12. The N.Y. Yankees move from the AFL and join the NFL. The league now consists of N.Y. Giants, N.Y. Yankees, Green Bay Packers, Chicago Bears, Chicago Cardinals, Cleveland Bulldogs, Providence Steam Roller, Frankford Yellow Jackets, Pottsville Maroons, Dayton Triangles, Duluth Eskimos and Buffalo Bisons.

The N.Y. Giants finish first (11-1-1) with the NFL's best defense (10 shutouts and 3 TDs scored against). Steve Owen and Cal Hubbard are standouts on the line.

Benny Friedman (Cleveland Bulldogs) tosses 12 TD passes and gains 1,700 yds in the air.

The N.Y. Giants beat the Chicago Bears in a key game at the Polo Grounds, 13-6. The Bears finish 3d (9-3-2) behind the Giants and Green Bay.

NFL All-Star Team
E: Lavie Dilweg (Green Bay), Cal Hubbard (N.Y. Giants)
T: Gus Sonnenberg (Providence), Ed Weir (Frankford, Pa.)
G: Mike Michalske (N.Y. Yankees), Steve Owen (N.Y. Giants)
C: Clyde Smith (Cleveland)
B: Benny Friedman (Cleveland), Vern Lewellen (Green Bay), Paddy Driscoll (Chicago Bears), Ernie Nevers (Duluth)

COLLEGE BOWL GAMES

ROSE BOWL:
   Stanford 7, Pittsburgh 6
Winning its first Rose Bowl game after three attempts, Pop Warner's Stanford team comes from behind to score its lone TD in the 3d quarter, followed by the all-important conversion. After a scoreless first half, Pittsburgh registers a TD in the 3d quarter when Stanford's fumble is picked up by Pittsburgh halfback Hagan, who dashes 19 yds into the end zone. Stanford ties the game later in that period as Wilton, whose earlier fumble led to Pittsburgh's TD, snatches a fumble made by his teammate Sims on the Pittsburgh 3-yd line and runs in for the score. Hoffman boots the ball through the uprights for the crucial extra point. Pittsburgh is coached by Jock Sutherland, who once played under Stanford coach Warner at Pittsburgh.

1928

COLLEGE REGULAR SEASON

The Big Six Conference (later known as the Big Eight) is established at a meeting in Lincoln, Neb. Founding members are Iowa State, Kansas, Kansas State, Missouri, Nebraska and Oklahoma.

Undefeated Georgia Tech scores 201 points during the season and gives up only 41 to lead the nation.

At halftime during the Army-Notre Dame game at Yankee Stadium, N.Y. (Nov. 10), coach Knute Rockne tells his Notre Dame players of the deathbed statement in 1920 of George Gipp, All-American back for Notre Dame (see *1920*): "When the breaks are beating the boys, tell them to go in there and win just one for the Gipper." Thus inspired, the Fighting Irish go on to upset previously undefeated Army, 12-6 (but lose the following week to Carnegie Tech and end the season with a 5-4 record, the worst in Rockne's career at Notre Dame).

Army and Navy sever athletic ties, as do Princeton and Harvard, ending (temporarily) their traditional rivalries.

Conference Champions
EAST: Boston College, Army, NYU, Carnegie Tech, Pennsylvania
BIG TEN: Illinois
BIG SIX: Nebraska
MISSOURI VALLEY: Drake
SOUTHWESTERN: Texas
PACIFIC COAST: USC

1928 All-American Team
E: Wes Fesler (Ohio State), Irv Phillips (California)
T: Mike Getto (Pittsburgh), Otto Pommerening (Michigan)
G: Seraphim Post (Stanford), Edward Burke (Navy)
C: Pete Pund (Georgia Tech)
B: Howard Harpster (Georgia Tech), Red Cagle (Army), Paul Scull (Pennsylvania), Ken Strong (New York University)

PROFESSIONAL REGULAR SEASON

Duluth, Cleveland and Buffalo drop out of the NFL, while the Detroit Wolverines are added, leaving 10 teams.

Providence Steam Roller, coached by Jimmy Conzelman, surprises the NFL with an 8-1-2 record. Tailback Wildcat Wilson and Curly Oden are the offensive stars. Gus Sonnenberg, Clyde Smith and Milt Rehnquist stand out on defense.

Benny Friedman (Detroit) leads the NFL in scoring (55 points) and rushes for more than 1,000 yds. But the Detroit franchise is forced to quit in mid-season because of poor gate receipts after running up a 7-2-1 record.

Ernie Nevers, after two sensational years at Duluth, quits the team and becomes assistant football coach at Stanford (his alma mater).

Jim Thorpe, 41, returns to play (1 game only) for the Chicago Cardinals, who lose 34-0. It is the last appearance in uniform for the NFL's first president and future Hall of Famer.

NFL All-Star Team
E: Lavie Dilweg (Green Bay), Ray Flaherty (N.Y. Giants)
T: Bill Owen (Detroit), Bull Behman (Frankford, Pa.)
G: Mike Michalske (N.Y. Yankees), Jim McMillin (Chicago Bears)
C: Clyde Smith (Providence)
B: Benny Friedman (Detroit), Wildcat Wilson (Providence), Verne Lewellen (Green Bay), Wally Diehl (Frankford, Pa.)

COLLEGE BOWL GAMES

ROSE BOWL:
Georgia Tech 8, California 7
During the 2d period, California's center and captain-elect Roy Riegels picks up a Georgia Tech fumble and races 60 yds toward the wrong goal. Finally, California halfback Benny Lom tackles his errant teammate on their own 3-yd line. Moments later, Georgia Tech tries to punt its way out of danger. The kick is blocked and bounces out of the end zone for an automatic touchback and 2 points for Georgia Tech, which eventually account for its margin of victory. Georgia Tech moves ahead, 8-0, in the 3d quarter on a 15-yd run by halfback Stumpy Thomason. California's only score comes late in the 4th quarter when left end Irv Phillips grabs a short pass from quarterback Lom. The extra-point kick is good, making the score close, 8-7, but not close enough.

COLLEGE REGULAR SEASON

Yale travels south of the Mason/Dixon line for the first time to help the University of Georgia dedicate its new football stadium. The Georgia Bulldogs shock the Yale Bulldogs, winning 15-0.

Notre Dame completes a perfect season (9 wins, no losses) without playing a game at home (their new stadium is under construction).

Army plays its first post-season game at Stanford and loses before 70,000 fans, 34-14.

Pittsburgh and Colgate are the top teams in the East. Purdue wins the Big Ten Conference; and on the Pacific Coast there is a 4-way tie between Stanford, California, Oregon and USC.

1929 All-American Team
E: Joe Donchess (Pittsburgh), Wes Fesler (Ohio State)
T: Bronko Nagurski (Minnesota), Elmer Sleight (Purdue)
G: Jack Cannon (Notre Dame), Ray Montgomery (Pittsburgh)
C: Ben Ticknor (Harvard)
B: Frank Carideo (Notre Dame), Red Cagle (Army), Gene McEver (Tennessee), Ralph Welch (Purdue)

PROFESSIONAL REGULAR SEASON

The Boston Bulldogs rejoin the NFL. Other new franchises include the Orange (N.J.) Tornadoes, Staten Island Stapletons and Minneapolis Redjackets. Gone from the league are Pottsville Maroons, N.Y. Yankees and Detroit Wolverines.

Coach Curly Lambeau (Green Bay) signs All-Stars Cal Hubbard and Mike Michalske, plus Johnny Blood (ex-Pottsville and Duluth member). Halfbacks Verne Lewellen, Bo Melenda and Blood each gain over 400 yds rushing. Defense allows only 3 TDs in 13 games (including 8 shutouts) as the Packers win their first NFL championship with a 12-0-1 record.

Tim Mara, N.Y. Giants owner, buys out the entire Detroit Wolverines squad, including All-Pro quarterback Benny Friedman, who tosses 20 TD passes and gains 1,500 yds in the air, enabling the Giants to move from 6th to 2d in the NFL standings.

Red Grange returns to the Chicago Bears and rushes for 552 yds.

Ernie Nevers returns to the Chicago Cardinals and leads the team in rushing, passing and scoring (including 40 points scored against the Chicago Bears, an NFL record).

NFL All-Star Team
E: Lavie Dilweg (Green Bay), Ray Flaherty (N.Y. Giants)
T: Bull Behman (Frankford, Pa.), Bob Beattie (Orange, N.J.)
G: Mike Michalske (Green Bay), Milt Rehnquist (Providence)
C: Joe Westoupal (N.Y. Giants)
B: Benny Friedman (N.Y. Giants), Verne Lewellen (Green Bay), Tony Plansky (N.Y. Giants), Ernie Nevers (Chicago Cardinals)

COLLEGE BOWL GAMES

ROSE BOWL:
   USC 47, Pittsburgh 14
Undefeated Pittsburgh is shocked by USC before 70,000 fans in the most lopsided score since 1902, when Michigan beat Stamford, 49-0, in the first Tournament of Roses game. With a potent passing attack (287 yds) and using many substitutions (34 players see action), the Trojans reel off 26 unanswered points in the 1st half and coast the rest of the way. Quarterback Saunders stars for USC, tossing 2 TD passes to Edelson.

1930

COLLEGE REGULAR SEASON

Army and Navy resume their rivalry after a two-year absence before a full house at Yankee Stadium in N.Y., with all proceeds going to the unemployed. Army wins, 6-0.

Notre Dame, led by All-American quarterback Frank Carideo, and Alabama are the nation's top-ranked teams. Both have perfect records.

In the East, Army, Colgate, Dartmouth and Fordham earn the best ratings.

Other Regional & Conference Champions
WESTERN CONFERENCE:
    Northwestern & Michigan
SOUTHERN CONFERENCE:
    Alabama & Tulane
BIG SIX: Kansas
PACIFIC COAST: Washington State
SOUTHWEST: Texas
ROCKY MOUNTAINS: Utah

1930 All-American Team
E: Wes Fesler (Ohio State), Frank Baker (Northwestern)
T: Fred Sington (Alabama), Milo Lubratovich (Wisconsin)
G: Barton Koch (Baylor), Ted Beckett (California)
C: Ben Ticknor (Harvard)
B: Frank Carideo (Notre Dame), Marchy Schwartz (Notre Dame), Erny Pinckert (USC), Leonard Macaluso (Colgate)

PROFESSIONAL REGULAR SEASON

New Brooklyn, Portsmouth and Newark franchises join the NFL, replacing Orange, Dayton, Boston and Buffalo.

Green Bay (10-3-1) wins its second straight championship by a narrow margin over the N.Y. Giants (13-4-0). Bo Melenda and Verne Lewellen both rush over 400 yds. Lewellen also gains 497 yds passing and scores 7 TDs rushing.

Rookie Bronko Nagurski, All-American from Minnesota, makes his debut with the Chicago Bears, combining with Red Grange for 541 yds rushing and 8 TDs.

Benny Friedman (N.Y. Giants) passes for more than 1,000 yds for the fourth year in a row.

Chris "Red" Cagle, ex-Army star, joins the N.Y. Giants and draws 45,000 fans to the Polo Grounds for a game with Green Bay.

The N.Y. Giants beat Knute Rockne's Notre Dame team, 22-0, in an exhibition match at the Polo Grounds before 55,000.

Ironton (Ohio) Tanks, an independent team coached by Greasy Neale and starring Glenn Presnell, defeats several NFL teams, including the Chicago Bears and N.Y. Giants.

NFL All-Star Team
E: Lavie Dilweg (Green Bay), Luke Johnson (Chicago Bears)
T: Jap Douds (Providence and Portsmouth), Link Lyman (Chicago Bears)
G: Mike Michalske (Green Bay), Walt Kiesling (Chicago Cardinals)
C: Swede Hagberg (Brooklyn)
B: Benny Friedman (N.Y. Giants), Red Grange (Chicago Bears), Ken Strong (Staten Island), Ernie Nevers (Chicago Cardinals)

COLLEGE BOWL GAMES

ROSE BOWL:
Alabama 24, Washington State 0
Wearing all-red uniforms, including shoes and socks, designed to match their reputation as the "Red Devils," the Cougars of Washington State gain lots of attention but lose to the Crimson Tide by a wide margin. Before a crowd of 70,000, Alabama is led by coach Wallace Wade. It is his last game at Alabama before taking over the reins at Duke. His players rise to the occasion, scoring 3 TDs in the 2d quarter to put the game beyond Washington State's reach. The first TD comes on a surprise end-around pass play, with end Moore hitting second-string halfback Suther on a long TD toss. Another substitute back, Campbell, accounts for the other 2 TDs, scampering 44 yds for one and crashing over from the 1-yd line for the other. Whitworth's field goal for Alabama in the 3d quarter is the only score in the 2d half. Washington State's only scoring threat ends on the Alabama 1-yd line when the Cougar captain, Schwartz, fumbles the ball away moments before the final gun sounds.

COLLEGE REGULAR SEASON

Knute Rockne, Notre Dame's legendary coach, dies in an airplane crash while en route to California.

Tulane ends its regular season undefeated, allowing only 21 points scored against it, then loses to USC in the Rose Bowl. USC thus becomes the national college football champion for 1931.

Harvard's only loss is to Yale, 3-0, as Albie Booth kicks a field goal for the win. Yale's only loss is to Georgia, while Army's sole defeat is to Harvard. The Cadets beat Navy, 17-7.

Michigan leads in the Midwest, losing only to Ohio State.

1931 All-American Team
E: Jerry Dalrymple (Tulane), Vernon Smith (Georgia)
T: Jesse Quatse (Pittsburgh), Dallas Marvil and Jack Riley (Northwestern)
G: Biggie Munn (Minnesota), John Baker (USC)
C: Tommy Yarr (Notre Dame)
B: Barry Wood (Harvard), Marchy Schwartz (Notre Dame), Gus Shaver (USC), Pug Rentner (Northwestern)

PROFESSIONAL REGULAR SEASON

The Minneapolis Redjackets and the Newark Tornadoes drop out of the NFL. The Cleveland Indians enter the league, leaving a total of 10 teams.

Green Bay (12-2-0) wins its 3d straight NFL title, with the Portsmouth Spartans a close second (11-3-0). The Packers score the most points (291) and give up only 87.

Portsmouth running backs Glenn Presnell (obtained from Ironton Tanks) and rookie Dutch Clarke combine for 948 yds rushing and 882 yds passing.

Red Grange (Chicago Bears) leads the league in rushing (599 yds). Johnny Blood (Green Bay) is the top receiver and scorer (84 points).

The Frankford Yellowjackets quit the NFL on Nov. 10 because of financial problems. Cleveland and the Providence Steam Roller also drop out of the NFL (at end of season), victims as well of the Depression in the early 1930s.

NFL All-Star Team
E: Red Badgro (N.Y. Giants), Lavie Dilweg (Green Bay)
T: George Christensen (Portsmouth), Cal Hubbard (Green Bay)
G: Butch Gibson (N.Y. Giants), Mike Michalske (Green Bay)
C: Frank McNally (Chicago Cardinals)
B: Red Grange (Chicago Bears), Ernie Nevers (Chicago Cardinals), Dutch Clark (Portsmouth), Johnny Blood (Green Bay)

COLLEGE BOWL GAMES

ROSE BOWL:
  USC 21, Tulane 12
USC captures its 3d Rose Bowl game in 10 years before 83,000 fans. The Trojans' All-American halfback, Ernie Pinckert, a blocking back throughout his playing career, is switched to a running back for the game and scores 2 touchdowns, using the only running play he knows: the reverse. Tulane's star runner, Glover, and left end Haynes bring their team back from a 21-0 deficit, each scoring a TD in the 2d half. Tulane outgains USC in all departments but is unable to take advantage of several scoring opportunities.

1932

COLLEGE REGULAR SEASON

Colgate finishes the season undefeated, untied and unscored upon.

The Southeastern Conference is formed, including Alabama, Auburn, Florida, Georgia, Georgia Tech, Kentucky, Louisiana State, Mississippi, Mississippi State, Sewanee, Tennessee, Tulane and Vanderbilt. Tennessee and Auburn each wins 9 out of 10 games (including a tie in their own head-to-head meeting) to lead the pack.

Pittsburgh is undefeated but tied by Ohio State and Nebraska. The Panthers are invited to the Rose Bowl. Michigan, led by quarterback Harry Newman, wins the Big Ten crown.

Other Conference Champions

BIG SIX: Nebraska
SOUTHWEST: Texas Christian
ROCKY MOUNTAIN: Utah
MISSOURI VALLEY: Oklahoma A&M
PACIFIC COAST: USC

1932 All-American Team

E: Paul Moss (Purdue), Joe Skladany (Pittsburgh)
T: Joe Kurth (Notre Dame), Ernie Smith (USC)
G: Milt Summerfelt (Army), Bill Corbus (Stanford)
C: Pete Gracey (Vanderbilt)
B: Warren Heller (Pittsburgh), Harry Newman (Michigan), Jimmy Hitchcock (Auburn), Don Zimmerman (Tulane)

PROFESSIONAL REGULAR SEASON

The Cleveland Indians, Providence Steam Roller and Frankford Yellowjackets drop out of the NFL.

George Preston Marshall reorganizes the Boston franchise, calling it the "Boston Braves." The new team produces the top NFL runner, Cliff Battles (576 yds rushing).

The NFL seeks to encourage more scoring (and prevent so many scoreless ties) by bringing the goal posts back to the goal line (beginning in 1933). The league also decides to make 2 divisions (East and West), with a postseason game deciding the championship (starting in 1933).

1931 champion Green Bay Packers meet the N.Y. Giants at the Polo Grounds (N.Y.) in a key game played before 30,000 fans. Giants (2-5-1) produce the year's biggest upset, winning 6-0.

The playoff game, forced indoors by poor weather, is played in Chicago Stadium (the field is only 45 yds wide and 60 yds long). With Dutch Clarke, star Portsmouth runner and passer, unable to play, the Bears beat the Spartans easily and capture their 2d NFL championship.

NFL All-Star Team

E: Luke Johnson (Chicago Bears), Ray Flaherty (N.Y. Giants)
T: Cal Hubbard (N.Y. Giants), Turk Edwards (Boston Braves)
G: Zuck Carlson (Chicago Bears), Walt Kiesling (Chicago Cardinals)
C: Nate Barrager (Green Bay)
B: Dutch Clarke (Portsmouth), Arnie Herber (Green Bay), Jack McBride (N.Y. Giants), Bronko Nagurski (Chicago Bears)

COLLEGE BOWL GAMES

ROSE BOWL:
 USC 35, Pittsburgh 0
Coach Jock Sutherland's Pittsburgh Panthers, still undefeated (but tied), face coach Howard Jones' unbeaten Trojans for the mythical national championship. What promises to be a close game turns into a rout, as USC repeats its upset win over Pittsburgh in the 1929 Rose Bowl. The Trojan defense, led by All-American tackle Ernie Smith, proves too strong for Pittsburgh's high-powered attack with All-American quarterback Warren Heller in charge. USC finishes the season with a perfect 10-0-0 record.

1933

COLLEGE REGULAR SEASON

Whittier College reserve player, Richard Nixon, completes his first season of college football.

Princeton goes undefeated, scoring 217 points to their opponents' 8.

Clipping, or blocking from behind the defender, is ruled illegal by the NCAA.

After losing 5 games, Notre Dame salvages its season with a 1-point victory over undefeated Army.

Conference Champions
BIG TEN: Michigan
BIG SIX: Nebraska
PACIFIC COAST: Stanford, Oregon, USC (3-way tie)
SOUTHEAST: Alabama
SOUTHERN: Duke

1933 All-American Team
E: Paul Geisler (Centenary), Joe Skladany (Pittsburgh)
T: Fred Crawford (Duke), Francis Wistert (Michigan)
G: Aaron Rosenberg (USC), Bill Corbus (Stanford)
C: Chuck Bernard (Michigan)
B: Cotton Warburton (USC), Pug Lund (Minnesota), Beattie Feathers (Tennessee), George Sauer (Nebraska)

PROFESSIONAL REGULAR SEASON

NFL
The NFL is now split into two 5-team divisions—East and West. Goal posts are moved back to the goal lines to encourage more scoring (via field goals). Passing is allowed anywhere behind the line of scrimmage (instead of the previous minimum 5 yds). The football itself is slimmed down to its modern shape.

Eastern Division Winner: New York (11-3-0). Giants win easily in the first year of the two-divison league. Ken Strong is the team's top runner and kicker, and rookie quarterback Harry Newman leads the NFL in passing (973 yds and 11 TDs). Coach Steve Owen, Mel Hein and Ray Flaherty are the defensive stars.

Western Division Winner: Chicago Bears (10-2-1). Coach George Halas leads the Bears to their first division title. Defense is led by rookie George Musso, Bill Hewitt and Joe Kopcha, allowing only 82 points scored against in 13 games. Halfback Bronko Nagurski rushes for 533 yds.

League Leaders: *Passer:* Benny Friedman (Brooklyn); *Rusher:* Jim Musick (Boston); *Receiver:* Paul Moss (Pittsburgh Pirates); *Scorer:* Glenn Presnell (Portsmouth).

COLLEGE BOWLS & PRO CHAMPIONSHIPS

College Bowl Games
ROSE BOWL:
   Columbia 7, Stanford 0
Columbia star Al Barabas scores the only TD on a hidden-ball play in a big upset on a rain-soaked field.
ORANGE BOWL:
   Duquesne 33, Miami 7
Michigan (7-0-1) is named national college champion for 1933.

NFL Championship Game
   Chicago 23, New York 21
Down 7-6 at halftime, the Bears score 17 points in the 2d half to win the NFL's first championship game. In the 1st half, Chicago's Jack Manders kicks 2 field goals and Red Badgro scores on a 29-yd pass from Harry Newman for the Giant score. Manders boots his 3d field goal in the 3d quarter, but N.Y. regains the lead on a TD by Max Krause. Bronko Nagurski's pass to Bill Karr puts Chicago in the lead, but the Giants answer with Newman's 4th quarter TD pass to Ken Strong. The final (and winning) Bears' score follows a pass from Newman to Bill Hewitt, who laterals to Karr, who races 36 yds for the TD.

1934

COLLEGE REGULAR SEASON

Undefeated Minnesota, led by All-American fullback Pug Lund, is named national college football champion, piling up 270 points to its opponents' 38.

Future U.S. President Gerald Ford is named the most outstanding player in the Michigan squad.

Pittsburgh leads the East, losing only to Minnesota. Colgate, beaten only by Ohio State, is the runner-up.

Navy beats Army, 3-0, for the first time since 1921. The Midshipmen's only loss is to Pittsburgh. Army, which outscores its rivals, 215 to 40, loses 3 games by a total of 16 points.

Conference Champions
BIG TEN: Minnesota
SOUTHEASTERN: Alabama
PACIFIC COAST: Stanford

1934 All-American Team
E: Frank Larsen (Minnesota), Don Hutson (Alabama)
T: Bill Lee (Alabama), Bob Reynolds (Stanford)
G: Les Hartwig (Pittsburgh), George Barclay (North Carolina)
C: Darrell Lester (Texas Christian)
B: Bobby Grayson (Stanford), Fred Borries (Navy), Bill Wallace (Rice), Pug Lund (Minnesota)

PROFESSIONAL REGULAR SEASON

NFL
Eastern Division Winner: New York (8-5-0). Giants repeat as NFL East champs. Defense stars are Mel Hein, Butch Gibson, Bill Morgan and Red Badgro. Rookie quarterback Ed Danowski replaces injured Harry Newman in mid-season and remains the #1 quarterback for the next 7 years. Ken Strong, one of NFL's best defensive backs, also leads the offense in running and kicking.
Western Division Winner: Chicago (13-0-0). The powerful Bears enjoy the first perfect record in NFL history. Rookie back Beattie Feathers leads the league with 1,004 yds rushing behind the blocking of Bronko Nagurski. Feathers and Nagurski account for 15 TDs. The defense is headed by Joe Kopcha, Bill Hewitt, Link Lyman, George Musso and Bill Karr.

The Detroit Lions celebrate their first year in the NFL by winning 10 games in a row (including 7 shutouts) before losing to Green Bay, 3-0. A loss to the Bears by 3 points in the last game of the season costs the Lions the NFL West title.
League Leaders: *Passer:* Arnie Herber (Green Bay); *Rusher:* Beattie Feathers (Chicago); *Receiver:* Red Badgro (New York); *Scorer:* Dutch Clark (Detroit).

COLLEGE BOWLS & PRO CHAMPIONSHIPS

College Bowl Games
ROSE BOWL:
    Alabama 29, Stanford 13
Future Hall of Famer (for Green Bay) Don Hutson catches 6 passes from Dixie Howell, including 2 TDs.
SUGAR BOWL:
    Tulane 20, Temple 14
This was the first Sugar Bowl game.
ORANGE BOWL:
    Bucknell 26, Miami (Fla.) 0
Minnesota (8-0-0) and Alabama (10-0-0) are named national college champions for 1934.

NFL Championship Game
New York 30, Chicago 13.
The Giants avenge the 1933 defeat, beating the previously undefeated Bears on a frozen turf at the Polo Grounds. Chicago leads at the half, 10-3, on Bronko Nagurski's TD and Jack Manders' field goal. Ken Strong boots a field goal for the Giants. Manders' 2d field goal in the 3d quarter puts the Bears ahead, 13-3. The Giants, now wearing sneakers instead of regular cleats, ram across 4 quick TDs in the 4th quarter in a dramatic turnaround. Ed Danowski throws a 20-yd pass to Ike Franklin, Ken Strong races for 2 TDs and Danowski scores the final TD on a 6-yd run.

The first annual college All-Star football game is played in Chicago before 79,000 fans. The All-Stars hold the professional Chicago Bears to a scoreless tie.

COLLEGE REGULAR SEASON

Jay Berswanger, University of Chicago halfback, is the first recipient of the Heisman Trophy. Monk Meyer of Army and Bill Shakespeare of Notre Dame are runners-up.

Minnesota (8-0-0) and Southern Methodist (12-1-0) are named co-national college champions for 1935.

Only three teams—Minnesota, Princeton and Southern Methodist—are undefeated in regular season play.

At Durham, N.C., unbeaten North Carolina is upset by Duke before the largest crowd ever to see a football game in the South (46,880).

Conference Champions
BIG TEN: Minnesota
SOUTHEASTERN: Louisiana State
SOUTHWEST: Southern Methodist
IVY LEAGUE: Princeton
PACIFIC COAST: Stanford

1935 All-American Team
E: Gaynell Tinsley (Louisiana State), Bill Shuler (Army)
T: Larry Lutz (California), Dick Smith (Minnesota)
G: John Weller (Princeton), Paul Tangora (Northwestern)
C: Darrell Lester (Texas Christian)
B: Riley Smith (Alabama), Jay Berswanger (Chicago), Bobby Wilson (Southern Methodist), Bobby Grayson (Stanford)

PROFESSIONAL REGULAR SEASON

NFL
Eastern Division Winner: New York (9-3-0). The Giants take their 3d straight division title. Their defense (notably Mel Hein, Potsy Jones, Red Badgro and Bill Morgan) allows the fewest points (96) in the NFL East. Ed Danowski is the top ranked quarterback, with 11 TD passes and 795 yds in pass completions. Kink Richards replaces Ken Strong (retired) as the leading rusher, and rookie Tod Goodman is the top receiver.

In Philadelphia, coach Lud Wray, desperate to improve the Eagles' fortunes, hires rookie Alabama Pitts out of Sing Sing prison. The Eagles still finish last.

Western Division Winner: Detroit (7-3-2). The Lions replace the Bears as the NFL West winner. Dutch Clark, Ace Gutowsky and Ernie Caddel rush for a total of 1,157 yds and 12 TDs. Caddel also leads the team in pass receiving.

In Green Bay, the Packers introduce a promising rookie from Alabama: Don Hutson. He snares 18 passes for 420 yds and 7 TDs in his first season.

League Leaders: *Passer:* Ed Danowski (New York); *Rusher:* Doug Russell (Chicago Cardinals); *Receiver:* Tod Goodwin (New York); *Scorer:* Dutch Clark (Detroit).

COLLEGE BOWLS & PRO CHAMPIONSHIPS

College Bowl Games
ROSE BOWL:
    Stanford 7, Southern Methodist 0
SUGAR BOWL:
    Texas Christian 3, Louisiana State 2
ORANGE BOWL:
    Catholic University 20, Mississippi 19

The first Sun Bowl is held at El Paso, Texas, on Jan. 1, 1936. Hardin-Simmons and New Mexico State play to a 14-14 tie.

NFL Championship Game
    Detroit 26, New York 7
The Lions take advantage of a muddy field and freezing rain to beat the defending NFL champs. In the 1st quarter, Ace Gutowsky of Detroit rushes for a TD and teammate Dutch Clark breaks loose for a 40-yd TD run. The Giants score their only TD in the 2d quarter on a 42-yd pass play from Ed Danowski to Ken Strong. The Lions clinch a victory with a 13-point 4th quarter. Ernie Caddel plunges over from the 4-yd line and Buddy Parker runs in from 9 yds out.

1936

COLLEGE REGULAR SEASON

Larry Kelley, Yale's All-American end, is awarded the 2d annual Heisman Trophy. Runners-up are Sam Francis (Nebraska) and Ray Buivid (Marquette).

Minnesota is named national college football champion for the 2d year in a row. The Gophers' only loss is to Northwestern. It is the first team to be so honored by the Associated Press. Louisiana State and Pittsburgh are ranked 2d and 3d.

A record crowd of 102,000 watches Navy defeat Army, 7- 0, in Philadelphia.

Conference Champions
BIG TEN: Minnesota
PACIFIC COAST: Washington
SOUTHERN: Louisiana State
SOUTHEASTERN: Alabama
IVY LEAGUE: Dartmouth

1936 All-American Team
E: Gaynell Tinsley (Louisiana State), Larry Kelley (Yale)
T: Ed Widseth (Minnesota), Averell Daniell (Pittsburgh)
G: Max Starcevich (Washington), Joe Routt (Texas A&M)
C: Mike Basrak (Duquesne)
B: Clint Frank (Yale), Ray Buivid (Marquette), Ace Parker (Duke), Sam Francis (Nebraska)

PROFESSIONAL REGULAR SEASON

NFL
Eastern Division Winner: Boston (7-5-0). The Redskins beat the N.Y. Giants, 14-0, in the final game of the season to capture the title. Turk Edwards, Rick Concannon and Jim Musick lead the defense. Cliff Battles heads the offense along with Riley Smith. Owner George Marshall, angry at the poor support of Boston fans, moves the championship game (see next column) to New York and later transfers the franchise to Washington, D.C.
Western Division Winner: Green Bay (10-1-1). The Packers grab the title with the passing combo of Arnie Herber to Don Hutson (34 completions and 8 TDs). Clark Hinkle is the leading rusher (476 yds). Frank Butler, Lou Gordon, Walt Kiesling and Ernest Smith lead the defense.

In Chicago, 3 rookies—Ray Nolting, Joe Stydahar and Danny Fortmann—give promise of a future Bears' dynasty as they compile a 9-3-0 record.
League Leaders: *Passer:* Arnie Herber (Green Bay); *Rusher:* Ernie Caddel (Detroit); *Receiver:* Don Hutson (Green Bay); *Scorer:* Dutch Clark (Detroit).

COLLEGE BOWLS & PRO CHAMPIONSHIPS

College Bowl Games
ROSE BOWL:
  Pittsburgh 21, Washington 0
SUGAR BOWL:
  Santa Clara 21, LSU 14
COTTON BOWL:
  Texas Christian 16, Marquette 6
In the first Cotton Bowl, L.D. Meyer, son of TCU head coach Dutch Meyer, leads the Horned Frogs to victory, scoring all 16 points on 2 TD receptions, an extra point and a field goal.
ORANGE BOWL:
  Duquesne 13, Mississippi State 12

NFL Championship Game
Green Bay 21, Boston 6
With the game played on a neutral field by the request of Boston owner George Marshall, the Redskins are given a slim chance against the high-scoring Packers. Still, Boston trails by only a point at the half, following TDs by Green Bay's Don Hutson (43-yd toss from Arnie Herber) and Boston's Pug Rentner (1-yd plunge). The Packers go ahead in the 3d quarter on Herber's 2d TD pass (to Milt Gantenbein) and clinch the win in the 4th quarter on Bob Monnett's 2- yd plunge following a blocked punt.

COLLEGE REGULAR SEASON

Clint Frank, Yale's premiere All-American halfback, wins the Heisman Trophy. Byron "Whizzer" White of Colorado and Marshall Goldberg of Pittsburgh finish 2d and 3d in the balloting.

Led by halfback Bob McLeod, Dartmouth goes undefeated, finishing ahead of Yale, Harvard and Cornell in the informal Ivy League.

Pittsburgh, paced by its great running back Marshall Goldberg, is the top college team in the nation, beating out California, Fordham (which holds Pittsburgh to a scoreless tie) and Alabama (which is undefeated and untied).

Conference Champions
BIG TEN: Minnesota
PACIFIC COAST: California
SOUTHEASTERN: Alabama
SOUTHWEST: Rice
SOUTHERN: North Carolina
ROCKY MOUNTAIN: Colorado
IVY LEAGUE: Dartmouth

1937 All-American Team
E: Chuck Sweeney (Notre Dame), Jerome Holland (Cornell)
T: Ed Franco (Fordham), Tony Matisi (Pittsburgh)
G: Joe Routt (Texas A&M), Leroy Monsky (Alabama)
C: Clark Hinkle (Vanderbilt)
B: Clint Frank (Yale), Byron White (Colorado), Marshall Goldberg (Pittsburgh), Sam Chapman (California)

PROFESSIONAL REGULAR SEASON

NFL
Eastern Division Winner:
Washington (8-3-0). The Redskins, transferred from Boston by owner George Marshall, retain the division title, defeating the N.Y. Giants in the final game of the regular season, 49-14. Rookie quarterback Sammy Baugh sets the NFL on fire, completing 81 passes for 1,127 yds. Charley Malone is his top receiver. Cliff Battles leads in rushing with 874 yds and 5 TDs.

Western Division Winner:
Cleveland Rams join NFL West in 1937. Chicago (9-1-1). The Bears lose only to Green Bay to regain the NFL West title. The defense, led by Joe Stydahar, George Musso and Danny Fortmann, allows only 100 total points. Their solid running game features Bronko Nagurski, Ray Nolting and Jack Manders.

League Leaders: *Passer:* Sammy Baugh (Washington); *Rusher:* Cliff Battles (Washington); *Receiver:* Don Hutson (Green Bay); *Scorer:* Jack Manders (Chicago).

COLLEGE BOWLS & PRO CHAMPIONSHIPS

College Bowl Games
ROSE BOWL:
California 13, Alabama 0
SUGAR BOWL:
Santa Clara 6, Lousiana State 0
COTTON BOWL:
Rice 28, Colorado 14
Colorado jumps out to an early 14-0 lead as its All-American back, Byron "Whizzer" White, future U.S. Supreme Court associate justice and All-Pro at Pittsburgh, throws a TD pass and returns an interception 47 yds for a TD.
ORANGE BOWL:
Auburn 6, Michigan State 0
Texas Christian is named the 1937 national collegiate champion.

NFL Championship Game
Chicago 28, Washington 21
The Redskins score 21 points in the 3d quarter to clinch their first NFL championship. The Bears move in front in the 1st half on 2 TDs by Jack Manders (10-yd rush and a 39-yd pass from Bernie Masterson). Rookie quarterback Sammy Baugh tosses 3 TD passes in the 3d quarter (2 to Wayne Millner and 1 to Ed Justice), to gain a total of 358 yds. The Bears' vaunted running game is held to 150 yds.

1938

COLLEGE REGULAR SEASON

Texas Christian, Tennessee and Duke dominate the college football season. Duke ends its year unscored upon. The 1937 national champion, Pittsburgh, is upset by Carnegie Tech, 20-10, spoiling its season.

USC defeats Notre Dame in the final week of the season and wins the Rose Bowl nomination despite losses to Alabama and Washington early in the season.

Carnegie Tech is ranked #1 in the East, followed by Pittsburgh, Holy Cross, Cornell, Fordham, Dartmouth and Villanova.

Minnesota leads the Midwest after its defeat of Michigan, 7-6. It is Michigan's only loss under its new coach, Fritz Crisler, formerly of Princeton.

Davey O'Brien of Texas Christian is named the Heisman Trophy winner, beating out Marshall Goldberg of Pittsburgh, Bob McLeod of Dartmouth and Sid Luckman of Columbia.

Conference Champions
BIG TEN: Minnesota
BIG SIX: Oklahoma
PACIFIC COAST: California & USC
SOUTHWEST: Texas Christian
SOUTHEASTERN: Tennessee
SOUTHERN: Duke

1938 All-American Team
E: Jerome Holland (Cornell), Waddy Young (Oklahoma)
T: Ed Beinor (Notre Dame), Al Wolff (Santa Clara)
G: Ralph Heikkenen (Michigan), Ed Bock (Iowa State)
C: Ki Aldrich (Texas Christian)
B: Davey O'Brien (Texas Christian), Parker Hall (Mississippi), John Pingel (Michigan), Marshall Goldberg (Pittsburgh)

PROFESSIONAL REGULAR SEASON

NFL
Eastern Division Winner: New York (8-2-1). Giants replace the Redskins as NFL East title holders, trouncing the 1937 champions, 36-0. Ed Danowski passes for 84 yds on 70 completions. Jim Lee Howell is his leading receiver. Tuffy Leemans and Hank Soar are the team's top rushers. Center and linebacker Mel Hein is named the league's MVP. Ed Widseth and Cliff Johnson anchor the best defense in the NFL (only 79 points scored against).
Western Division Winner: Green Bay (8-3-0). The Packers discover a new star tailback: Cecil Isbell. He leads the team in rushing and passing (1,104 yds). Ace receiver Don Hutson is lost in mid-season to injury but still leads the NFL with 32 receptions for 548 yds and 9 TDs. Potsy Jones, Frank Butler and Moose Mulleneaux lead the defense.
League Leaders: *Passer:* Ed Danowski (New York); *Rusher:* Whizzer White (Pittsburgh); *Receiver:* Don Hutson (Green Bay); *Scorer:* Clarke Hinkle (Green Bay).

COLLEGE BOWLS & PRO CHAMPIONSHIPS

College Bowl Games
ROSE BOWL:
 USC 7, Duke 3
USC scores the game's only TD with only 41 seconds left to beat Duke. They are the only points scored against Duke throughout the 1938 season.
SUGAR BOWL:
 Texas Christian 15, Carnegie Tech 7
COTTON BOWL:
 St. Mary's 20, Texas Tech 13
ORANGE BOWL:
 Tennessee 17, Oklahoma 0

NFL Championship Game
New York 23, Green Bay 17
Giants win their 2d NFL championship, moving ahead 16-14 at halftime on Ward Cuff's field goal and TDs by Tuffy Leeman and Hap Barnard (20-yd pass from Ed Danowski). The Packers go ahead in the 3d quarter on Tiny Engebretsen's field goal, but the Giants clinch the win on a 23-yd TD pass play from Danowski to Hank Soar. Two blocked punts in the 1st quarter help the Giants. The Packers push across their only TDs in the 2d quarter on Clarke Hinkle's 1-yd rush and Moose Mulleneaux's catch of Arnie Herber's 40-yd toss.

COLLEGE REGULAR SEASON

Nile Kinnick of Iowa receives the Heisman Trophy. Tom Harmon of Michigan and Paul Christman of Missouri are runners-up.

The University of Chicago, one of the game's pioneers, drops football at the end of the 1939 season in response to the school's policy of de-emphasizing its athletic program.

Texas A&M is named the country's best college team, followed by Tennessee, USC, Cornell and Tulane. All are undefeated. Tennessee, which is unscored upon, extends its unbeaten string to 23 games (15 of which are won by shutouts).

Dr. Eddie Anderson, Iowa's new head coach, is named "Coach of the Year" after leading his team from last place in the Big Ten in 1938 to within 1 point of the title.

Cornell's perfect season is highlighted by its upset win over Ohio State in an intersectional match.

Conference Champions
BIG TEN: Ohio State
SOUTHWEST: Texas A&M
SOUTHEASTERN: Tennessee,
  Tulane & Georgia Tech (tie)
SOUTHERN: Duke & Clemson (tie)
BIG SIX: Missouri
PACIFIC COAST: USC
IVY LEAGUE: Cornell

All-American Team
E: Paul Severin (North Carolina), Buddy Kerr (Notre Dame)
T: Harley McCollum (Tulane), Nick Drahos (Cornell)
G: Harry Smith (USC), Ed Molinski (Tennessee)
C: John Schiechl (Santa Clara)
B: Nile Kinnick (Iowa), Tom Harmon (Michigan), Banks McFadden (Clemson), John Kimbrough (Texas A&M)

PROFESSIONAL REGULAR SEASON

NFL
Eastern Division Winner: New York (9-1-1). The Giants retain their division title with a good defense that allows only 85 points scored against it in 11 games. Their only loss is to Detroit by 4 points. New York's secondary intercepts a league-high 35 passes. The offense is led by Tuffy Leemans, Ed Danowski and kicker Ward Cuff; the line is anchored by Mel Hein, Frank Cope, Jim Poole and Johnny Dell Isola.
Western Division Winner: Green Bay (9-2-0). The Packers take their 2d straight NFL West title. Don Hutson has his best year with 34 receptions for 846 yds and 6 TDs. Cecil Isbell runs and passes for 1,156 yds. Green Bay's front line features Russ Letlow and Buckets Goldenberg.

In Chicago, rookie quarterback Sid Luckman comes out of Columbia University to lead the Bear offense. He and fullback Bill Osmanski produce 1,335 yds in their first full season.
League Leaders: *Passer:* Frank Filchock (Washington); *Rusher:* Bill Osmanski (Chicago); *Receiver:* Don Hutson (Green Bay); *Scorer:* Andy Farkas (Washington).

COLLEGE BOWLS & PRO CHAMPIONSHIPS

College Bowl Games
ROSE BOWL:
  USC 14, Tennessee 0
After going through the regular season undefeated, untied and unscored upon, the Vols of Tennessee are shut out by the Trojans in the Rose Bowl (Jan. 1, 1940).
SUGAR BOWL:
  Texas A&M 14, Tulsa 13
COTTON BOWL:
  Clemson 6, Boston College 3
ORANGE BOWL:
  Georgia Tech 21, Missouri 7
In the first Blue-Gray game between North and South seniors, North wins, 7-0, at Montgomery, Ala. (Jan. 2, 1939).

NFL Championship Game
  Green Bay 27, New York 0
The Packers administer the first shutout in NFL championship game history. The only score in the first half is on a short pass from Arnie Herber to Milt Gantenbein. The Packers score 4 times in the 2d half on 2 field goals and TDs by Joe Laws (on a pass from Cecil Isbell) and Ed Jankowski (1-yd plunge). Green Bay's secondary picks off 6 Giant passes and its defense allows only 79 yds rushing. Ed Danowski, veteran Giant passer, completes 4 out of 12 for 48 yds, while Tuffy Leemans, New York's top runner, picks up 24 yds in 12 tries.

Bronko Nagurski of the Chicago Bears takes a handoff and heads upfield.
UPI/NFL Photos

Ernie Nevers, one of Stanford's all-time greats and later a professional All-Star.
Pro Football Hall of Fame/NFL Photos

Byron "Whizzer" White, former All-American at Colorado, all-round star for the Pittsburgh Pirates of the NFL, and future justice of the U.S. Supreme Court.
NFL Photos

George Halas, a charter member of the Professional Football Hall of Fame and coach of the Chicago Bears from 1921 to 1968.
NFL Photos

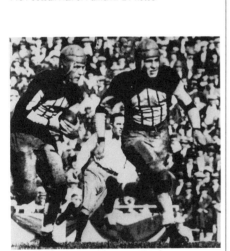

Red Grange, the "Galloping Ghost" of Illinois, carries the ball for another big gain.
World Wide Photos/NFL Photos

Mel Hein, great center for the N.Y. Giants, moves in to nail the ball carrier.
World Wide Photos/NFL Photos

COLLEGE REGULAR SEASON

The first college game ever presented on TV is played between Maryland and Pennsylvania (Oct. 5).

Tom Harmon of Michigan breaks the 15-year-old scoring record of Red Grange and is later named winner of the Heisman Trophy. John Kimbrough (Texas A&M) and George Franck (Minnesota) finish 2d and 3d in the balloting.

Minnesota, undefeated and untied, is named the top college team, followed by Stanford, Michigan, Tennessee, Boston College, Texas A&M, Nebraska, Northwestern, Mississippi State and Washington.

Cornell, ranked #1 in the country for the first 4 weeks of the season, is upset by Dartmouth after having apparently won the game, 7 to 3. A review of the game film shows that Cornell scored its winning TD on an illegal 5th down. The Cornell score is disallowed and Dartmouth wins, making this the first time a score has been reversed in college football.

Conference Champions
BIG TEN: Minnesota
BIG SIX: Nebraska
SOUTHEASTERN: Tennessee
SOUTHWEST: Texas A&M &
   Southern Methodist (tie)
IVY LEAGUE: Pennsylvania

1940 All-American Team
E: Paul Severin (North Carolina), Buddy Elrod (Mississippi State)
T: Nick Drahos (Cornell), Bob Reinhard (California)
G: Bob Suffridge (Tennessee), Warren Alfson (Nebraska)
C: Chet Gladchuck (Boston College)
B: Frankie Albert (Stanford), Tom Harmon (Michigan), George Franck (Minnesota), John Kimbrough (Texas A&M)

PROFESSIONAL REGULAR SEASON

NFL
Eastern Division Winners:
Washington (9-2-0). The Redskins beat out the Brooklyn Dodgers by 1 game for the title (N.Y. Giants drop to 3d). Sammy Baugh is the top NFL passer with a 63% completion rate (1,367 yds and 12 TDs). Dick Todd catches 20 passes for 402 yds and rushes for 408 yds.

Art Rooney, owner of the Pittsburgh Steelers, sells his team at the end of the season, then decides to buy back the franchise (with Bert Bell as co-owner and coach) during off-season.

Western Division Winner:
Chicago (8-3-0). Sid Luckman takes charge of the Bear offense, featuring Joe Maniaci, Bill Osmanski, Jack Manders, Ray Nolting and Gary Famiglietti. Their combined rushing yardage (1,818) is best in the NFL. Rookies include halfback George McAfee, end Ken Kavanaugh, tackles Lee Artoe and Ed Kolman and center Bulldog Turner.

League Leaders: *Passer:* Sammy Baugh (Washington); *Rusher:* Whizzer White (Detroit); *Receiver:* Don Looney (Philadelphia); *Scorer:* Don Hutson (Green Bay).

COLLEGE BOWLS & PRO CHAMPIONSHIPS

College Bowl Games
ROSE BOWL:
   Stanford 21, Nebraska 13
SUGAR BOWL:
   Boston College 19, Tennessee 13
COTTON BOWL:
   Texas A&M 13, Fordham 12
ORANGE BOWL:
   Mississippi State 14, Georgetown 7

NFL Championship Game
Chicago 73, Washington 0
Having defeated the Bears 7-3 just 3 weeks earlier, the Redskins go into the NFL championship game with confidence. Instead, they suffer the worst defeat in NFL history. The score at halftime is 28-0 following TDs by Bill Osmanski on a 68-yd jaunt on the 2d play of the game, a quarterback sneak by Sid Luckman, Joe Maniaci's 42-yd run and rookie Ken Kavanaugh's catch of Luckman's 30-yd toss in the 2d quarter. Chicago goes on to score 4 TDs in the 3d quarter and 3 more in the final quarter. In all, Chicago's offense rolls up 391 yds rushing and 138 yds passing. The Redskins are held to 55 yds on the ground. Chicago's secondary intercepts 8 passes to halt Washington's vaunted air game.

COLLEGE REGULAR SEASON

Minnesota, led by All-American halfback Bruce Smith, is voted the nation's top team for the 2d year in a row, running its unbeaten streak to 17. Duke, Notre Dame, Texas, Michigan, Fordham, Missouri, Duquesne, Texas A&M and Navy round out the top 10. Minnesota also wins its 8th Big Ten title under head coach Bernie Bierman.

Minnesota's star halfback, Bruce Smith, edges out Angelo Bertelli of Notre Dame and Frankie Albert of Stanford for the Heisman Trophy.

Minnesota's star halfback, Bruce Smith, edges out Angelo Bertelli of Notre Dame and Frankie Albert of Stanford for the Heisman Trophy.

Don Faurot, Missouri coach, introduces the split-T formation, featuring a sliding, ball-handling quarterback. Free substitutions are now permitted (except in the final 2 minutes of the half). Substitutes may also bring in plays from the bench.

Conference Champions
BIG TEN: Minnesota
SOUTHWEST: Texas A&M
BIG SIX: Missouri
PACIFIC COAST: Oregon State
SOUTHERN: Duke
SOUTHEASTERN: Mississippi State
ROCKY MOUNTAIN: Utah

1941 All-American Team
E: Dave Schreiner (Wisconsin), Mal Kutner (Texas)
T: Dick Wildung (Minnesota), Bob Reinhard (California)
G: Endicott Peabody (Harvard); Ralph Fife (Pittsburgh)
C: Darrell Jenkins (Missouri)
B: Frankie Albert (Stanford), Bill Dudley (Virginia), Frank Sinkwich (Georgia), Bruce Smith (Minnesota)

PROFESSIONAL REGULAR SEASON

NFL
Eastern Division Winner: New York (8-3-0). The Giants win their 6th division title, losing the first game of the season to Brooklyn, 16-13, on Dec. 7 following public announcement of the attack on Pearl Harbor. Tuffy Leemans takes over as the team's leading passer and runner (807 total yds). Ward Cuff is the top receiver and kicker. New York's defense allows the fewest points in the NFL (114). Rookie guard Len Younce is a standout along with Mel Hein, Monk Edwards, Frank Cope and others.

Western Division Winner: Chicago (10-1-0). The Bears and Packers each lose only one game during the season—to each other. The Bears win the playoff game, 33-14, to win their division title. Sid Luckman is the league's best passer with a 57% completion rate and only 6 interceptions during the season. George McAfee and Hugh Gallarneau are Chicago's top rushers. McAfee also intercepts 6 passes on defense, returns punts and catches passes.

League Leaders: *Passer:* Sid Luckman (Chicago); *Rusher:* George McAfee (Chicago); *Receiver:* Don Hutson (Green Bay); *Scorer:* Don Hutson (Green Bay).

COLLEGE BOWLS & PRO CHAMPIONSHIPS

College Bowl Games
ROSE BOWL:
   Oregon State 20, Duke 16
The Rose Bowl game is transferred from Pasadena to Durham, N.C., due to the threat of an enemy air attack on the West Coast.
SUGAR BOWL:
   Fordham 2, Missouri 0
COTTON BOWL:
   Alabama 29, Texas A&M 21
Alabama gains only 1 first down but takes advantage of 7 interceptions and 5 fumble recoveries to win the game.
ORANGE BOWL:
   Georgia 40, Texas Christian 26
Frank Sinkwich of Georgia throws 3 TD passes and runs for a 4th TD.

NFL Championship Game
   Chicago 37, New York 9
The Bears retain their NFL title before a small crowd caused by the December 7 attack on Pearl Harbor. Bob Snyder boots 3 field goals to give Chicago the early lead, 9-6. After Ward Cuff ties the game with a field goal, the Bears score 4 straight TDs, 2 on short rushes by Norm Standlee, another by George McAfee, and Ken Kavanaugh's 42-yd return of a Giant fumble. The Giant offense is held to 84 yds rushing and 73 yds passing. The Bears recover 2 fumbles and intercept 3 New York passes.

1942

COLLEGE REGULAR SEASON

The Army-Navy game is seen by only 12,000 fans as the government restricts wartime ticket sales to residents within 10 miles of the stadium.

UCLA's star halfback and future Baseball Hall of Famer Jackie Robinson catches a 46-yd TD pass in the annual College All-Star game against the Chicago Bears.

Frank Sinkwich, Georgia quarterback, is named the Heisman Trophy winner, beating out Paul Governali (Columbia) and Otto Graham (Northwestern).

WWII produces several outstanding service teams, including the Army All-Stars, Great Lakes Naval Training and the Iowa Seahawks. Freshmen are made eligible to play on college varsities because of the manpower shortage. Wartime travel restrictions also affect schedules and attendance adversely.

Ohio State is named the top team in college football, followed by Georgia, Wisconsin, Tulsa (the nation's only major unbeaten team), Georgia Tech, Notre Dame, Tennessee, Boston College, Michigan and Alabama.

Conference Champions
WESTERN (BIG TEN): Ohio State
SOUTHEASTERN: Georgia
SOUTHERN: William & Mary
SOUTHWEST: Texas
BIG SIX: Missouri
PACIFIC COAST: UCLA

1942 All-American Team
E: Dave Schreiner (Wisconsin), Bob Shaw (Ohio State)
T: Dick Wildung (Minnesota), Clyde Johnson (Kentucky)
G: Garrard Ramsey (William & Mary), Chuck Taylor (Stanford)
C: Joe Domnanovich (Alabama)
B: Glenn Dobbs (Tulsa), Paul Governali (Columbia), Frank Sinkwich (Georgia), Mike Holovak (Boston College)

PROFESSIONAL REGULAR SEASON

NFL
Eastern Division Winner:
Washington (10-1-0). The Redskins' only loss is to the N.Y. Giants, 14-7, in the 2d game of the season. Washington's defense yields 102 points and the fewest yds rushing (848) in the NFL East. Sammy Baugh leads all passers with a 58% completion rate. Andy Farkas is the top rusher as many of the league's stars leave for military service.
Western Division Winner:
Chicago (11-0-0). With coach George Halas called back to Navy duty, the Bears still repeat their perfect season of 1934. Sid Luckman and Charlie O'Rourke have a combined passing yardage of 1,974 on 96 completions. Gary Famiglietti is the top rusher (503 yds and 8 TDs). Chicago's defense gives up only 84 points and 519 yds, best in the NFL. [Note: Cecil Isbell of Green Bay is the first man in NFL history to pass for more than 2,000 yds in one season.]
League Leaders: *Passer:* Cecil Isbell (Green Bay); *Rusher:* Bill Dudley (Pittsburgh); *Receiver:* Don Hutson (Green Bay); *Scorer:* Don Hutson (Green Bay).

COLLEGE BOWLS & PRO CHAMPIONSHIPS

College Bowl Games
ROSE BOWL:
  Georgia 9, UCLA 0
SUGAR BOWL:
  Tennessee 14, Tulsa 7
COTTON BOWL:
  Texas 14, Georgia Tech 7
ORANGE BOWL:
  Alabama 37, Boston College 21

NFL Championship Game
Washington 14, Chicago 6
The Redskins gain some revenge for the 73-0 beating by Chicago in the 1940 championship game. The Bears score first on Lee Artoe's 52-yd return of a Redskin fumble. Washington takes the lead at halftime on a 39-yd pass from quarterback Sammy Baugh to Wilbur Moore. The only score in the 2d half comes on a 1-yd plunge by Washington's Andy Farkas. The Bears' running attack is held to 102 yds as neither team is able to move the ball effectively.

COLLEGE REGULAR SEASON

Quarterback Angelo Bertelli of Notre Dame is named the Heisman Trophy winner, beating out Bob Odell of Pennsylvania and Otto Graham of Northwestern.

Notre Dame is selected as the top college team in the nation, despite a loss to Great Lakes Naval Training Station in the final 30 seconds of play on a 46-yd TD pass. The other top-10 teams include Iowa Pre-Flight, Michigan, Navy, Purdue, Great Lakes, Duke, Del Monte Pre-Flight, Northwestern and March Field.

Army drops its 5th game in a row to Navy, 13-0. The game is played at West Point for the first time since 1892.

Amos Alonzo Stagg, 81-year-old coach at College of the Pacific and one of football's leading pioneers, is named "Coach of the Year."

Conference Champions
WESTERN (BIG TEN): Michigan
SOUTHERN: Duke
SOUTHEAST: Georgia Tech
SOUTHWESTERN: Texas
MISSOURI VALLEY: Tulsa
BIG SIX: Oklahoma
PACIFIC COAST: USC

1943 All-American Team
E: Joe Parker (Texas), Ralph Heywood (USC)
T: Jim White (Notre Dame), Pat Preston (Duke)
G: John Steber (Georgia Tech), George Brown (Navy)
C: Casimir Myslinsky (Army)
B: Angelo Bertelli (Notre Dame), Creighton Miller (Notre Dame), Otto Graham (Northwestern), Bill Daley (Michigan)

PROFESSIONAL REGULAR SEASON

NFL
Eastern Division Winner: [Note: Due to war, the Pittsburgh Steelers and Philadelphia Eagles merge for the 1943 season, leaving the NFL Eastern Division with only 4 teams.] Washington (6-3-1). After compiling a 6-0-1 record, the Redskins lose their last 3 games and end the season tied with New York. Washington wins the playoff game, 28-0. Sammy Baugh's 56% completion rate is the best in the NFL. His favorite receivers are Wilbur Moore and Joe Aguirre. Baugh also leads the NFL in interceptions (11). Top Redskin defenders are Leon Rymkus, Willie Wilkin and George Smith.
Western Division Winner: [Note: The Cleveland Rams withdraw from the league for 1943 because of the manpower shortage.] Chicago (8-1-1). Bronko Nagurski comes out of retirement to lead the wartime Bears to their 4th straight division title. Their only loss is to Washington. Sid Luckman is ranked the NFL's top passer. Harry Clark gains 1,091 yds (including 10 TDs) as a runner and receiver.
League Leaders: *Passer:* Sid Luckman (Chicago); *Rusher:* Bill Paschal (New York); *Receiver:* Don Hutson (Green Bay); *Scorer:* Don Hutson (Green Bay).

COLLEGE BOWLS & PRO CHAMPIONSHIPS

College Bowl Games
ROSE BOWL:
  USC 20, Washington 0
SUGAR BOWL:
  Georgia Tech 20, Tulsa 18
COTTON BOWL:
  Randolph Field 7, Texas 7
ORANGE BOWL:
  Louisiana State 19, Texas A&M 14

NFL Championship Game
Chicago 41, Washington 21
Sid Luckman fires 5 TD passes and runs 54 yds to lead the Bears to their 3d NFL championship in 4 years. Ahead 14-7 at the half, the Bears break loose with 27 points in the 2d half. Washington's star, Sammy Baugh, completes 2 TD passes after missing most of the game with a mild concussion. The Bears intercept 4 passes and limit the Redskin runners to 50 yds.

COLLEGE REGULAR SEASON

Despite a severe shortage of talent, college football endures during the war years with young, less experienced players. Army is the outstanding team of the year, rolling up 504 points (an average of 56 per game) and winning all 9 games on its schedule. The Cadet defense holds the opposition to 35 points (3.9 per game).

The other top 10 teams in the nation are Ohio State, Navy, USC, Michigan, Notre Dame, Duke, Tennessee, Georgia Tech and Illinois.

The Heisman Trophy goes to Les Horvath, Ohio State quarterback. Runners-up are Army's great backfield duo of Doc Blanchard and Glenn Davis.

Conference Champions
WESTERN (BIG TEN): Ohio State
PACIFIC COAST: USC
SOUTHERN: Duke
SOUTHEASTERN: Georgia Tech
SOUTHWEST: Texas Christian
BIG SIX: Oklahoma
MISSOURI VALLEY: Oklahoma A&M

1944 All-American Team
E: Pete Tinsley (Georgia Tech), Hub Bechtol (Texas)
T: Don Whitmire (Navy), John Ferraro (USC)
G: Bill Hackett (Ohio State), Hamilton Nichols (Rice)
C: Calebdan Warrington (Auburn)
B: Les Horvath (Ohio State), Glenn Davis (Army), Bob Fenimore (Oklahoma A&M), Doc Blanchard (Army)

PROFESSIONAL REGULAR SEASON

NFL
The Boston Yanks join the NFL East in 1944. The Philadelphia Eagles "divorce" the Pittsburgh Steelers after a 1-yr merger.

Eastern Division Winner: New York (8-1-1). Arnie Herber, former Green Bay star, joins New York after a 3-year retirement and leads the team to its 7th NFL East title. New York's defense produces 5 shutouts and allows only 75 points. Bill Paschal rushes for a league-high 737 yds and 9 TDs.

Western Division Winner: The Cleveland Rams rejoin the NFL West. The Chicago Cardinals and Pittsburgh Steelers merge for the 1944 season.

Green Bay (8-2-0). Irv Comp replaces Cecil Isbell and leads the Packers to their 4th division title (coach Curley Lambeau's last). Don Hutson grabs 58 passes for 866 yds and 9 TDs to lead all receivers for the 4th straight year.

League Leaders: *Passer:* Frankie Filchock (Washington); *Rusher:* Bill Paschal (N.Y.); *Receiver:* Don Hutson (Green Bay); *Scorer:* Don Hutson (Green Bay).

COLLEGE BOWLS & PRO CHAMPIONSHIPS

College Bowl Games
ROSE BOWL:
   USC 25, Tennessee 0
This is USC's 8th straight Rose Bowl win.
SUGAR BOWL:
   Duke 29, Alabama 26
Leading 26-20 late in the 4th quarter, Alabama elects to take an intentional safety and then kick from its own 20-yd line. But the plan backfires when Duke roars back with a 20-yd TD run for a last-minute TD and 29-26 triumph.
COTTON BOWL:
   Oklahoma A&M 34, Texas Christian 0
ORANGE BOWL:
   Tulsa 26, Georgia Tech 12

NFL Championship Game
   Green Bay 14, New York 7
In a game dominated by defense, 2 TDs in the 2d quarter are all the Packers need to win. Ted Fritsch goes over from the 1-yd line, then catches a 28-yd pass from Irv Comp for the 2d score. The Giants' only TD comes in the 4th quarter on Ward Cuff's 1-yd plunge (New York's star running back, Bill Paschal, is unable to play most of the game because of an ankle injury). Packers' interceptions of 4 Arnie Herber passes, plus 90 yds in penalties against N.Y., also help Green Bay.

COLLEGE REGULAR SEASON

Army, featuring its star running backs Doc Blanchard and Glenn Davis, dominates college football for the 2d year in a row. The Cadets' unbeaten string is extended to 18, marking the first time Army has enjoyed two successive seasons without a defeat. The final game against once-beaten Navy (won by Army, 32-13) draws a crowd of 100,000.

Other top 10 teams include Alabama, Navy, Indiana, Oklahoma A&M, Michigan, St. Mary's (Calif.), Pennsylvania, Notre Dame and Texas. Indiana wins the Western Conference (Big Ten) title for the first time in 46 years and is undefeated for the first time in its history.

Fullback Doc Blanchard of Army wins the Heisman Trophy. Teammate Glenn Davis and Bob Fenimore (Oklahoma A&M) are runners-up.

Conference Champions
SOUTHEASTERN: Alabama
SOUTHERN: Duke
IVY LEAGUE: Pennsylvania
WESTERN: Indiana
BIG SIX: Missouri
SOUTHWEST: Texas
PACIFIC COAST: USC
BIG SEVEN (formerly Rocky Mountain): Denver

1945 All-American Team
E: Hub Bechtol (Texas), Dick Duden (Navy)
T: DeWitt Coulter (Army), Al Nemetz (Army)
G: John Green (Army), Warren Amling (Ohio State)
C: Vaughn Mancha (Alabama)
B: Herman Wedemeyer (St. Mary's), Bob Fenimore (Oklahoma A&M), Glenn Davis (Army), Doc Blanchard (Army)

PROFESSIONAL REGULAR SEASON

NFL
Eastern Division Winner: Washington (8-2-0). Redskins capture their 5th NFL East title behind a record-breaking performance by quarterback Sammy Baugh (70.3% pass completion rate). Kicker Joe Aguirre boots 7 field goals and 23 out of 24 PATs. Frank Akins rushes for 797 yds and 6 TDs.

Western Division Winner: [Note: Although Green Bay does not win a division title, its top receiver and kicker, Don Hutson, sets an all-time record for points scored in one quarter by snaring 4 TD passes and kicking 5 PATs for a total of 29 pts.] Cleveland Rams (9-1-0). In their final season in Cleveland before moving to L.A., the Rams win their only division title behind rookie quarterback Bob Waterfield, who passes for 1,609 yds and 14 TDs. Top receiver is Jim Benton (1,067 yds and 8 TDs). Waterfield (husband of film star Jane Russell) also punts, kicks extra points and plays defense (6 interceptions).

NFL's longest losing streak (29 games) ends when the Chicago Cardinals defeat the Chicago Bears (Oct. 14).

League Leaders: *Passer:* Sammy Baugh (Washington); *Rusher:* Steve Van Buren (Philadelphia); *Receiver:* Jim Benton (Cleveland); *Scorer:* Steve Van Buren (Philadelphia).

COLLEGE BOWLS & PRO CHAMPIONSHIPS

College Bowl Games
ROSE BOWL:
 Alabama 34, USC 14
SUGAR BOWL:
 Oklahoma A&M 33, St. Mary's 13
COTTON BOWL:
 Texas 40, Missouri 27
Bobby Layne passes for 2 TDs, scores 4 TDs, and kicks 4 extra points for the Texas Longhorns.
ORANGE BOWL:
 Miami 13, Holy Cross 6
With the score tied 6-6, Miami's Hudson intercepts a Holy Cross pass on the final play of the game and races 89 yds for a TD and 13-6 victory.

NFL Championship Game
Cleveland 15, Washington 14
The Rams head for their new home in Los Angeles with their first NFL championship clinched. The difference in the game is a freak safety caused when a pass thrown by Redskin quarterback Sammy Baugh from his own end zone in the 1st quarter hits the goal post. The Redskins take the lead on a 38-yd TD pass from Frank Filchock to Steve Bagarus. The Rams recapture the lead at the half on Bob Waterfield's 37-yd pass play to Jim Benton. Cleveland adds to its lead in the 3d quarter when Jim Gillette scores on a 53-yd pass from Waterfield. Filchock's toss to Bob Seymour narrows the gap to a point, but there is no further scoring.

1946

COLLEGE REGULAR SEASON

Army completes its 3d straight undefeated season but suffers a scoreless tie against Notre Dame. The traditional Army-Navy game nearly results in one of the greatest upsets in sports history. Down 21-6 at the half, Navy, loser of 7 straight games and a 28-point underdog, fights back to within 3 points of the Cadets. With the ball on Army's 3-yd line, Navy falls short of the winning TD as time runs out.

Notre Dame, led by quarterback Johnny Lujack, replaces Army as the #1 team in the nation. Other top 10 teams include Army, Illinois, Michigan, Tennessee, Louisiana State, North Carolina and Rice.

In a game against Temple, West Virginia attempts 18 passes and completes none.

Glenn Davis, Army's great running back, wins the Heisman Trophy. Charlie Trippi (Georgia) and Johnny Lujack (Notre Dame) finish 2d and 3d in the balloting.

Conference Champions
WESTERN (BIG TEN): Illinois
SOUTHEASTERN: Tennessee & Georgia
PACIFIC COAST: UCLA
SOUTHERN: North Carolina
SOUTHWEST: Rice & Arkansas

1946 All-American Team
E: Burr Baldwin (UCLA), Elmer Madar (Michigan)
T: George Connor (Notre Dame), Dick Huffman (Tennessee)
G: Weldon Humble (Rice), Alex Agase (Illinois)
C: Paul Duke (Georgia Tech)
B: Johnny Lujack (Notre Dame), Charlie Trippi (Georgia), Glenn Davis (Army), Doc Blanchard (Army)

PROFESSIONAL REGULAR SEASON

NFL
Bert Bell is named NFL Commissioner. Cleveland Rams move to Los Angeles. And a new league—All-American Football Conference (AAFC)—is organized. Also, the first black players are signed: Marion Motley and Bill Willis (AAFC) and Woody Strode (NFL).

Eastern Division Winner: New York (7-3-1). Quarterback Frank Filchock leads the Giants to the NFL East title. Jim Poole and Frank Liebel are his primary receivers.

Western Division Winner: Chicago (8-2-1). The Bears resume their pre-war leadership in the NFL West as their stars return from the armed forces, including backs Bill Osmanski and Hugh Gallarneau. Quarterback Sid Luckman continues to lead the offense with 110 completions, including 17 TDs.

League Leaders: *Passer:* Sid Luckman (Chicago); *Rusher:* Bill Dudley (Pittsburgh); *Receiver:* Jim Benton (Los Angeles); *Scorer:* Ted Fritsch (Green Bay).

AAFC
Eastern Division Winner: New York (10-3-1). The Yankees (formerly Brooklyn Tigers) are led by quarterback Ace Parker. Rookie running back Spec Sanders leads the AAFC in rushing (709 yds) and passes for 411 yds.

Western Division Winner: Cleveland (12-2-0). Led by quarterback Otto Graham, the Browns win a division title in their first season under coach Paul Brown. Marion Motley and "Special Delivery" Jones are the top running backs.

League Leaders: *Passer:* Glenn Dobbs (Brooklyn); *Rusher:* Spec Sanders (New York); *Receiver:* Dante Lavelli (Cleveland); *Scorer:* Lou Groza (Cleveland).

COLLEGE BOWLS & PRO CHAMPIONSHIPS

College Bowl Games
ROSE BOWL:
    Illinois 45, UCLA 14
Al Hoisch of UCLA, the smallest man on the field, returns a kickoff for a 103-yd TD (a Rose Bowl record). The Rose Bowl is now restricted to winners of the Big Nine Conference (now Big Ten) and Pacific Coast Conference (now Pacific-10).
SUGAR BOWL:
    Georgia 20, North Carolina 10
COTTON BOWL:
    Arkansas 0, LSU 0
ORANGE BOWL:
    Rice 8, Tennessee 0

NFL
Championship Game: Chicago 24, New York 14. Commissioner Bert Bell suspends Giant back Merle Hapes and quarterback Frank Filchock for failure to report bribe offers. Filchock is allowed to play in the championship game and throws 2 TD passes in a losing cause. Bear quarterback Sid Luckman passes for a TD and runs 19 yds for the winning score in the 4th quarter.

AAFC
Championship Game: Cleveland 14, New York 9. The Yankees score first on Harvey Johnson's field goal, but the Browns go ahead at the half on Marion Motley's 1-yd plunge. Following Spec Sanders' TD run in the 3d quarter, the Browns score the winning TD in the 4th quarter on quarterback Otto Graham's toss to Dante Lavelli.

COLLEGE REGULAR SEASON

After winning 32 games straight, Army loses to Columbia, 21-20, in a stunning upset. Army later loses to unbeaten Notre Dame, 27-7, which makes the Fighting Irish #1 in the nation.

Penn State goes undefeated for the first time since 1912 and wins the Lambert Trophy as best team in the East.

Michigan, led by All-American halfback Bob Chappuis, is also undefeated and captures the Western Conference (Big Ten) for the first time since 1933.

A new unlimited substitution rule makes it possible for more players to get into the game. It also fosters the use of offensive and defensive specialists, paving the way for "two-platoon" football.

Conference Champions
WESTERN (BIG TEN): Michigan
SOUTHERN: William & Mary
SOUTHWEST: Southern Methodist
IVY LEAGUE: Pennsylvania
SOUTHEASTERN: Mississippi
PACIFIC COAST: USC
BIG SIX: Oklahoma & Kansas
MISSOURI VALLEY: Tulsa
BIG SEVEN: Utah

1947 All-American Team
E: Paul Cleary (USC), Bill Swiacki (Columbia)
T: Bob Davis (Georgia Tech), Dick Harris (Texas)
G: Steve Suhey (Penn State), Bill Fischer (Notre Dame)
C: Chuck Bednarik (Pennsylvania)
B: Johnny Lujack (Notre Dame), Bob Chappuis (Michigan), Ray Evans (Kansas), Doak Walker (Southern Methodist)

PROFESSIONAL REGULAR SEASON

NFL
Eastern Division Winner: Philadelphia (8-4-0). The Eagles end their season tied with Pittsburgh. Philadelphia wins the playoff game, 21-0, to take the NFL East title. The offensive star is Steve Van Buren, who rushes for a record 1,008 yds in 12 games. Philadelphia's defense is the best in the NFL, allowing only 1,320 yds rushing.
Western Division Winner: Chicago (9-3-0). The Cardinals win their division title by beating crosstown rival Bears in the last game of the season. The Cardinal backfield of Paul Christman, Elmer Angsman, Charlie Trippi and Pat Harder is tops in the NFL.
League Leaders: *Passer:* Sammy Baugh (Washington); *Rusher:* Steve Van Buren (Philadelphia); *Receiver:* Mal Kutner (Chicago Cardinals); *Scorer:* Pat Harder (Chicago Cardinals).

AAFC
Eastern Division Winner: New York (11-2-1). Tailback Spec Sanders rushes for an AAFC record (1,432 yds) and passes for 1,442 yds, accounting for 32 TDs. Rookie halfback Buddy Young adds 849 yds rushing and receiving.
Western Division Winner: Cleveland (12-1-1). The Browns retain their division title, losing only to Los Angeles. Quarterback Otto Graham continues to lead the offense (and the AAFC) with 25 TD passes and 2,753 yds in the air. Marion Motley rushes for 889 yds behind a veteran line.
League Leaders: *Passer:* Otto Graham (Cleveland); *Rusher:* Spec Sanders (New York); *Receiver:* Mac Speedie (Cleveland); *Scorer:* Spec Sanders (New York).

COLLEGE BOWLS & PRO CHAMPIONSHIPS

College Bowl Games
ROSE BOWL:
    Michigan 49, USC 0
Forty-six years after beating Stanford in the first Rose Bowl, 49-0, Michigan makes its 2d appearance in the Rose Bowl and beats USC by the same score.
SUGAR BOWL:
    Texas 27, Alabama 7
COTTON BOWL:
    Southern Methodist 13, Penn State 13
ORANGE BOWL:
    Georgia Tech 20, Kansas 14
With the ball on Georgia Tech's 1-yd line and less than 2 minutes to play, Kansas quarterback Lynne McNutt fumbles the snap from center and Georgia Tech recovers to save the game.

NFL
Championship Game: Chicago 28, Philadelphia 21. Except for Charlie Trippi's 44-yd TD run in the 1st quarter for the Cardinals, the teams are dead even, matching TDs for 3 quarters. Trippi also runs back a punt 75 yds for a TD in the 3d quarter. The Cardinals outrush the Eagles, 282 yds to 60, including two 70-yd dashes by Elmer Angsman. The Eagles' Tommy Thompson passes for 297 yds in a losing cause.

AAFC
Championship Game: Cleveland 14, New York 3. The Browns beat the Yankees in the championship game for the 2d year in a row. Quarterback Otto Graham sneaks over for Cleveland's 1st score, and Special Delivery Jones runs over from 4 yds out in the 3d quarter. New York scores on Harvey Johnson's 12-yd field goal. Marion Motley of Cleveland leads all rushers with 109 yds.

COLLEGE REGULAR SEASON

Notre Dame and Michigan dominate U.S. college football. The Fighting Irish go undefeated for the third year in a row. Notre Dame narrowly misses losing to USC in the last game of the season, scoring a TD in the last minute of play for a 7-7 tie.

Michigan enjoys its second straight perfect season and is voted #1 in the country ahead of Notre Dame. Other top teams are North Carolina, California, Oklahoma and Army.

Doak Walker (Southern Methodist) leads in the balloting for the Heisman Trophy, beating out Chuck Bednarik of Pennsylvania and Charley Justice of North Carolina.

The Army-Navy game again provides a shocker for football fans. Having won all 8 games, Army manages only a tie (21-21) against Navy, loser of all 8 games it has played.

Conference Champions

BIG NINE (WESTERN CONFERENCE/BIG TEN): Michigan
SOUTHERN: Clemson
PACIFIC COAST: California & Oregon
SOUTHWEST: Southern Methodist
IVY LEAGUE: Cornell
MISSOURI VALLEY: Oklahoma A&M

1948 All-American Team

E: Dick Rifenburg (Michigan), Barney Poole (Mississippi)
T: Leo Nomellini (Minnesota), Bill Fischer (Notre Dame)
G: Paul Burris (Oklahoma), Rod Manz (California)
C: Chuck Bednarik (Pennsylvania)
B: Bobby Jack Stuart (Army), Doak Walker (Southern Methodist), Charley Justice (North Carolina), Art Murakowski (Northwestern)

PROFESSIONAL REGULAR SEASON

NFL

Eastern Division Winner: Philadelphia (9-2-1). The Eagles recapture the division title, winning 8 straight after an opening day loss to the Chicago Cardinals. Steve Van Buren leads all runners with 945 yds and 10 TDs. Tommy Thompson's passes to Pete Pihos and Jack Ferranti net 18 TDs.

Western Division Winner: Chicago (11-1-0). After losing to its crosstown rival Bears, the Cardinals win 10 in a row, beating the Bears 24-21 in the final game to clinch a division title. Quarterbacks Ray Mallouf and Paul Christman lead the passing attack. Halfbacks Charlie Trippi and Elmer Angsman, plus fullback Pat Harder, rush for 1,882 yds.

League Leaders: *Passer:* Sammy Baugh (Washington); *Rusher:* Steve Van Buren (Philadelphia); *Receiver:* Mal Kutner (Chicago Cardinals); *Scorer:* Pat Harder (Chicago Cardinals).

AAFC

Eastern Division Winner: Buffalo (7-7-0). Tied for the lead with the Baltimore Colts at the end of the regular season, the Bills win the division title in a playoff, 28-17. Quarterback George Ratterman leads the passing attack. Halfbacks Chet Mutryn and Lou Tomasetti rush for 1,539 yds.

Western Division Winner: Cleveland (14-0-0). The Browns complete their first undefeated season, led by 8 All-Conference players. Quarterback Otto Graham tosses 25 TD passes and Marion Motley gains 964 yds on the ground.

League Leaders: *Passer:* Y.A. Tittle (Baltimore); *Rusher:* Marion Motley (Cleveland); *Receiver:* Billy Hillenbrand (Baltimore); *Scorer:* Chet Mutryn (Buffalo).

COLLEGE BOWLS & PRO CHAMPIONSHIPS

College Bowl Games

ROSE BOWL:
Northwestern 20, California 14
SUGAR BOWL:
Oklahoma 14, North Carolina 6
COTTON BOWL:
Southern Methodist 21, Oregon 13
ORANGE BOWL:
Texas 41, Georgia 13

NFL

Championship Game: Philadelphia 7, Chicago 0. Played in a heavy snowstorm, the game is scoreless for 3 quarters. The Cardinals are held to 35 yds passing and 96 yds rushing, losing the ball twice on fumbles. Eagles' star runner Steve Van Buren rushes for 98 yds and scores the game's only TD in the 4th quarter. Quarterback Tommy Thompson of the Eagles completes only 2 passes for 7 net yds.

AAFC

Championship Game: Cleveland 49, Buffalo 7. The Bills are completely outclassed by the undefeated Browns, who roll up 215 yds rushing (Marion Motley gains 133 yds in 14 carries) and 118 yds passing. The Bills fumble 3 times and have 5 passes intercepted. Motley and "Special Delivery" Jones each score 2 TDs.

1949

COLLEGE REGULAR SEASON

Wyoming beats Colorado State College 103-0, a single-game record for most points scored by one team.

Coach Tom Nugent of Virginia Military Institute introduces the I-formation, featuring 3 backs lined up in a row behind the quarterback.

Notre Dame (ranked #1), Oklahoma, California and Army are the only major college teams with perfect records. Under coach Frank Leahy, Notre Dame has played 38 games without a loss. Army, under coach Earl "Red" Blaik, enjoys its 5th perfect season in 6 years. Others in the top 10 are Rice, Ohio State, Michigan, Minnesota, Louisiana State and College of the Pacific.

Leon Hart of Notre Dame is awarded the Heisman Trophy (only the second lineman to be so honored). Charley Justice (North Carolina) and Doak Walker (Southern Methodist) are runners-up.

Conference Champions
BIG NINE: Ohio State & Michigan
PACIFIC COAST: California
BIG SEVEN: Oklahoma
SOUTHWEST: Rice
SOUTHEASTERN: Tulane
SOUTHERN: North Carolina
IVY LEAGUE: Cornell

1949 All-American Team
E: Leon Hart (Notre Dame), Jim Williams (Rice)
T: Jim Martin (Notre Dame), Wade Walker (Oklahoma)
G: Rod Franz (California), John Schweder (Pennsylvania)
C: Clayton Tonnemaker (Minnesota)
B: Arnold Galiffa (Army), Doak Walker (Southern Methodist), Charley Justice (North Carolina), Emil Sitko (Notre Dame)

PROFESSIONAL REGULAR SEASON

NFL
Eastern Division Winner: Philadelphia (11-1-0). The Eagles keep their division title, losing only to the Chicago Bears. Using a 5-2-4 defense for the first time, the Eagle defense allows only 148 points during the season (30 by rushing). Halfback Steve Van Buren rushes for 1,146 yds and 11 TDs to lead the league. Quarterback Tommy Thompson throws 16 TD passes.
Western Division Winner: Los Angeles (8-2-2). The Rams win their first division title behind quarterbacks Bob Waterfield and rookie Norm Van Brocklin. "Crazy Legs" Hirsch catches 22 passes. He is the AAFC's first flanker, augmenting ends Tom Fears (77 receptions for 1,013 yds) and Bob Shaw.
League Leaders: *Passer:* Sammy Baugh (Washington); *Rusher:* Steve Van Buren (Philadelphia); *Receiver:* Bob Mann (Detroit); *Scorers:* Mel Harder (Chicago Cardinals) and Choo-Choo Roberts (New York) tied.

AAFC
The AAFC adopts a playoff system involving the top 4 teams:

Cleveland (9-1-2). The Browns' only loss is a 56-28 whipping by the San Francisco 49ers. Otto Graham continues as the AAFC's top quarterback. Mac Speedie is the top receiver (1,028 yds).

San Francisco (9-3-0). The 49ers' rout of Cleveland (56-28) is the high spot of their season.

New York (8-4-0). The Yankees lose star quarterback Spec Sanders (knee injury) and are forced to rely on a running game.

Buffalo (5-5-2). The Bills tie champion Cleveland twice, losing 3 other games by a total of 13 points.
League Leaders: *Passer:* Otto Graham (Cleveland); *Rusher:* Joe Perry (San Francisco); *Receiver:* Mac Speedie (Cleveland); *Scorer:* Alyn Beals (San Francisco).

COLLEGE BOWLS & PRO CHAMPIONSHIPS

College Bowl Games
ROSE BOWL:
Ohio State 17, California 14
SUGAR BOWL:
Oklahoma 35, LSU 0
COTTON BOWL:
Rice 27, North Carolina 13
ORANGE BOWL:
Santa Clara 21, Kentucky 12

NFL
Championship Game: Philadelphia 14, Los Angeles 0. The Eagles win their 2d straight championship in a rainstorm, shutting off the Rams' famed passing attack with only 10 completions for 98 yds, and allowing only 21 yds on the ground. Eagle halfback Steve Van Buren sets a rushing record of 196 yds. Philadelphia scores on Tommy Thompson's 31-yd pass to Pete Pihos and a blocked punt return by defensive end Leo Skledany.

AAFC
Playoffs: Cleveland 31, Buffalo 21; San Francisco 17, New York 7.
Championship Game: Cleveland 21, San Francisco 7. The Browns close out the AAFC with their 4th straight championship and look ahead to proving themselves in the NFL. A strong ground game (217 yds) and quarterback Otto Graham's leadership spark the Cleveland offense. Halfback "Special Delivery" Jones scores 2 TDs and fullback Marion Motley races 63 yds for a Cleveland TD in the 3d quarter.

1940-1950

Chuck Bednarik, Pennsylvania's All-American center and future pro star with the Philadelphia Eagles.

Sid Luckman, (far left), the pride of Columbia University and veteran quarterback for the Chicago Bears, discusses strategy with his coach, **George Halas** (right).
Nate Fine/NFL Photos

One of the great passers of all time, **Sammy Baugh** shows off the form that made him the best. Nate Fine/NFL Photos

Otto Graham, all-pro quarterback for the Cleveland Browns, fakes a hand-off before dropping back for a pass. Frank Rippon/NFL Photos

COLLEGE REGULAR SEASON

Jim Thorpe, former U.S. Olympic champion and All-American at Carlisle Indian School, is voted the greatest athlete of the half century (1900-1950).

In a blinding snowstorm, Michigan beats Ohio State, 9- 3, without making a first down or completing a pass, and with only 27 yds gained rushing.

The long winning streaks of Army and Notre Dame come to an end, with Oklahoma and Princeton the only major college teams to win all their games. The Sooners are rated #1, followed by Army, Texas, Tennessee, California, Princeton, Kentucky, Michigan, Michigan State and Clemson.

Conference Champions

BIG TEN: Michigan
BIG SEVEN: Oklahoma
IVY LEAGUE: Princeton
SOUTHWEST: Texas
SOUTHEASTERN: Kentucky
PACIFIC COAST: California

1950 All-American Team

(O = Offense; D = Defense)
E: Dan Foldberg (O-Army), Don Stonesifer (O-Northwestern), Frank Anderson (D-Oklahoma), Don Menasco (D-Texas)
T: Jim Weatherall (O-Oklahoma), Bob Gain (O-Kentucky), Al Carapella (D-Miami), Al Wahl (D-Michigan)
G: Lewis McFadin (O-Texas), Bob Ward (O-Maryland), Les Richter (D-California), Ted Daffer (D-Tennessee)
C: Bill Vohaska (O-Illinois)
L: Elmer Stout (D-Army), Irv Holdash (D-North Carolina)
B: Don Heinrich (O-Washington), Bob Reynolds (O-Nebraska), Everett Grandelius (O-Michigan State), Dick Kazmaier (O-Princeton), Bob Williams (D-Notre Dame), Vic Janowicz (D-Ohio State), Eddie Salem (D-Alabama)

PROFESSIONAL REGULAR SEASON

The All-American Football Conference (AAFC) is dissolved at the end of the 1949 season. The NFL picks up 3 former AAFC franchises: Cleveland, San Francisco and Baltimore.

NFL

American Conference Winner: Cleveland (10-2-0). In its first year in the NFL, Cleveland loses only to New York (twice) but gains revenge at the end of the season when it beats the Giants, 8- 3, in a playoff game. Quarterback Otto Graham leads the offense with pinpoint passes to Dante Lavelli, Mac Speedie and Dub Jones. Marion Motley rushes for 810 yds to lead the NFL. Cleveland's pass defense is the best in the league and stars Len Ford, Tommy James and Warren Lehr.
National Conference Winner: Los Angeles (9-3-0). The Rams repeat as division (now conference) champs, using a strong passing attack. Tied with Chicago at the end of the season, they take the playoff game, 24-14. Quarterbacks Norm Van Brocklin and Bob Waterfield throw 29 TD passes and gain 3,601 yds in the air. Tom Fears is the leading receiver (84 catches for 1,116 yds). Team totals of 64 TDs and 466 points in one season are NFL records.
League Leaders: *Passer:* Norm Van Brocklin (Los Angeles); *Rusher:* Marion Motley (Cleveland); *Receiver:* Tom Fears (Los Angeles); *Scorer:* Doak Walker (Detroit).

COLLEGE BOWLS & PRO CHAMPIONSHIPS

College Bowl Games

ROSE BOWL:
   Michigan 14, California 6
SUGAR BOWL:
   Kentucky 13, Oklahoma 7
Wilbur Jameson of Kentucky catches a 23-yd pass from Babe Parilli as the Wildcats upset Oklahoma and end the Sooners' 31-game winning streak.
COTTON BOWL:
   Tennessee 20, Texas 14
ORANGE BOWL:
   Clemson 15, Miami 14

NFL

Championship Game: Cleveland 30, Los Angeles 28. Rams quarterback Bob Waterfield hits former Army star Glenn Davis with an 82-yd pass play to set the tone of the championship game as the Browns, in their first year in the NFL, remain champions. Quarterback Otto Graham tosses 3 TD passes and gains 298 yds in the air. Behind 28-20 in the 4th quarter, Graham hits Rex Baumgardner with a 14-yd TD pass and Lou Groza kicks a 16-yd field goal with 28 seconds left in the game to win. L.A. quarterback Bob Waterfield gains 312 yds in the air, but 5 interceptions prove costly.

COLLEGE REGULAR SEASON

Tennessee (ranked #1), Michigan State, Maryland and Princeton (22 straight wins) are the only major teams with perfect records.

The NCAA approves the televising of college football on Saturday afternoons but restricts coverage to only 1 game in each area.

Once mighty Army, its team devastated by wholesale dismissals for honor code violations, wins only 2 games.

All-American halfback Dick Kazmaier of Princeton takes the Heisman Trophy, beating out Hank Lauricella (Tennessee) and Babe Parilli (Kentucky) by a wide margin.

Conference Champions
WESTERN (BIG TEN): Illinois
PACIFIC COAST: Stanford
SOUTHEASTERN: Tennessee & Georgia Tech
SOUTHERN: Maryland & Virginia Military Institute
SOUTHWEST: Texas Christian
BIG SEVEN: Oklahoma
MISSOURI VALLEY: Tulsa
IVY LEAGUE: Princeton

1951 All-American Team
(O = Offense; D = Defense)
E: Bill McColl (O-Stanford), Bob Carey (O-Michigan State), Pat O'-Donahue (D-Wisconsin), Dewey Mc-Connell (D-Wyoming)
T: Bob Toneff (O-Notre Dame), Don Coleman (O-Michigan State), Jim Weatherall (D-Oklahoma), Bill Pearman (D-Tennessee)
G: Bob Ward (O-Maryland), Marvin Matuszak (O-Tulsa), Ray Beck (D-Georgia Tech), Joe Palumbo (D-Virginia)
C: Doug Moseley (O-Kentucky)
LB: Keith Flowers (D-Texas Christian), Les Richter (D- California)
B: Dick Kazmaier (O-Princeton), Hank Lauricella (O- Tennessee), Hugh McIlhenny (O-Washington), Larry Isbell (O-Baylor), Bobby Dillon (D-Texas), Al Brosky (D-Illinois), Ollie Matson (D-San Francisco)

PROFESSIONAL REGULAR SEASON

NFL
American Conference Winner: Cleveland (11-1-0). After losing the opener to L.A., the Browns win 11 straight to keep the conference title. Quarterback Otto Graham, one of 9 All-Pros on the team, has his best year with 17 TD passes and 2,205 yds gained passing. Dante Lavelli, Mac Speedie and Dub Jones are his primary receivers. The defense allows the fewest points scored against any team (152) in the NFL.
National Conference Winner: Los Angeles (8-4-0). The only club to beat Cleveland, Los Angeles boasts 2 top-ranked quarterbacks, Norm Van Brocklin and Bob Waterfield. They combine for 26 TD passes and 188 completions. "Crazy Legs" Hirsch is their top receiver (65 catches for 1,495 yds and 17 TDs). Dick Towler is #1 running back (854 yds). Andy Robustelli, Woodley Lewis and Jerry Williams are standouts on defense.
League Leaders: *Passer:* Otto Graham (Cleveland); *Rusher:* Eddie Price (New York); *Receiver:* "Crazy Legs" Hirsch (Los Angeles); *Scorer:* "Crazy Legs" Hirsch (Los Angeles).

COLLEGE BOWLS & PRO CHAMPIONSHIPS

College Bowl Games
ROSE BOWL:
 Illinois 40, Stanford 7
SUGAR BOWL:
 Maryland 28, Tennessee 13
All-American halfback Hank Lauricella of Tennessee carries the ball 7 times for 1 net yard as the top-ranked Vols are upset.
COTTON BOWL:
 Kentucky 20, Texas Christian 13
ORANGE BOWL:
 Georgia Tech 17, Baylor 14

NFL
Championship Game: Los Angeles 24, Cleveland 17. Behind 10-7 at halftime, the Rams avenge their loss to Cleveland in the 1950 championship game. Both teams rely on strong passing attacks, with Cleveland's Otto Graham throwing for 280 yds and Bob Waterfield and Norm Van Brocklin combining for 253 yds. Tied 17-17 in the 4th quarter, L.A. wins on a 73-yd pass play from Van Brocklin to Tom Fears, who snares 4 passes in all for 146 yds.

1952

COLLEGE REGULAR SEASON

Michigan State and Georgia Tech have the only perfect records among major college teams. The Spartans stretch their undefeated string to 24 games and are named the top team in the country. Georgia Tech is ranked #2 after running their own winning streak to 25 games.

Notre Dame, despite losses to Pittsburgh and Michigan State, defeats conference champions Purdue (Western), USC (Pacific Coast), Oklahoma (Big Seven) and Texas (Southwest) to earn #3 ranking.

Halfback Billy Vessels (Oklahoma) is awarded the Heisman Trophy, with Jack Scarbath (Maryland) and Paul Giel (Minnesota) close behind.

Other Conference Champions
SOUTHERN: Duke
WESTERN: Wisconsin (tied with Purdue)
MISSOURI VALLEY: Houston
IVY LEAGUE: Pennsylvania

1952 All-American Team
(O = Offense; D = Defense)
E: Tom Stolhandske (O-Texas), Frank McPhee (O-Princeton), Don Branby (D-Colorado), Tom Scott (D-Virginia)
T: Kline Gilbert (O-Mississippi), Dave Suminski (O- Wisconsin), J.D. Kimmel (D-Houston), Charlie Lapradd (D-Florida)
G: John Miches (O-Tennessee), Marvin Matuszak (O-Tulsa), Frank Kush (D-Michigan State), Steve Eisenhauer (D-Navy)
C: Pete Brown (O-Georgia Tech)
LB: Richard Tamburo (D-Michigan State), Donn Moomaw (D-UCLA)
B: Billy Vessels (O-Oklahoma), Paul Giel (O-Minnesota), Don Heinrich (O-Washington), Jack Scarbath (O-Maryland), Jim Sears (D- USC), Johnny Lattner (D-Notre Dame), Bobby Moorhead (D-Georgia Tech)

PROFESSIONAL REGULAR SEASON

NFL
American Conference Winner: Cleveland (8-4-0). Despite losing 4 games (most in the club's history), the Browns capture their 4th conference title in a row. Quarterback Otto Graham's accurate passing (181 completions and 20 TD passes) and Mac Speedie's receptions (62 for 911 yds) lead the offense. Their defense is the best in the NFL against the pass (40.5% completion rate). Len Ford and Bill Willis are strong against the rush.

National Conference Winner: [Note: Dallas Texans replace the N.Y. Yanks in the NFL National Conference.] Detroit (9-3-0). The Lions win their first championship since 1935, defeating Los Angeles in a playoff game, 31-21. Quarterback Bobby Layne directs the offense, completing 139 passes for 1,999 yds. Receiver Cloyce Box snags 42 passes for 924 yds and 15 TDs (best in NFL). Yale Lary and Jack Christiansen are defensive stars along with Les Bingaman and Thurmon McGraw.

League Leaders: *Passer:* Tobin Rote (Green Bay); *Rusher:* Dan Towler (Los Angeles); *Receiver:* Billy Howton (Green Bay); *Scorer:* Gordie Soltau (San Francisco).

COLLEGE BOWLS & PRO CHAMPIONSHIPS

College Bowl Games
ROSE BOWL:
USC 7, Wisconsin 0
SUGAR BOWL:
Georgia Tech 24, Michigan 7
COTTON BOWL:
Texas 16, Tennessee 0
ORANGE BOWL:
Alabama 61, Syracuse 6
Alabama sets a single game scoring record in Big Four bowl play (Rose, Sugar, Cotton, Orange) with 61 points vs Syracuse.

NFL
Championship Game: Detroit 17, Cleveland 7. Although season statistics strongly favor Cleveland, the final score indicates the effects of injuries to key Cleveland players, plus a failure to capitalize on golden opportunities. After a scoreless 1st quarter, Bobby Layne puts Detroit ahead with a quarterback sneak. The Lions move further in front on Doak Walker's 67-yd dash in the 3d quarter. The Browns score their only points on a 7-yd run by Chick Jagade (who is the game's leading ground gainer with 104 yds). Lou "The Toe" Groza, Cleveland's ace kicker, plays with cracked ribs and misses 3 crucial field goal attempts.

COLLEGE REGULAR SEASON

The NCAA votes to abolish two-platoon football in favor of the old one-platoon system. A limited substitution rule is also imposed.

Navy beats Princeton, 65-7, for the Tigers' worst defeat in 85 years.

The undefeated strings of Georgia Tech (31 games) and Michigan State (28 games) come to an end during the 1953 season.

The Atlantic Coast Conference is formed and includes Clemson, Duke, Maryland, North Carolina, North Carolina State, South Carolina, Virginia and Wake Forest.

Maryland (10-0-0) is the only major college team with a perfect record and is ranked #1 in the nation. Others in the top 10 (in order) are Notre Dame, Michigan State, Oklahoma, UCLA, Rice, Illinois, Iowa, Georgia Tech and West Virginia.

Quarterback Johnny Lattner of Notre Dame wins the Heisman Trophy over Paul Giel (Minnesota) and Paul Cameron (UCLA).

Conference Champions
BIG TEN: Michigan State & Illinois
IVY LEAGUE: Cornell
ATLANTIC COAST: Duke & Maryland
SOUTHEASTERN: Alabama
PACIFIC COAST: UCLA
SOUTHERN: West Virginia
SOUTHWEST: Rice & Texas
BIG SEVEN: Oklahoma
MISSOURI VALLEY: Okalahoma A&M & Detroit

1953 All-American Team
E: Don Dohoney (Michigan State), Sam Morley (Stanford)
T: Stan Jones (Maryland), Jack Shanafelt (Pennsylvania)
G: J.D. Roberts (Oklahoma), Crawford Mims (Mississippi)
C: Larry Morris (Georgia Tech)
B: Paul Giel (Minnesota), Johnny Lattner (Notre Dame), Paul Cameron (UCLA), Kosse Johnson (Rice)

PROFESSIONAL REGULAR SEASON

NFL
Instead of "American Conference" and "National Conference," the NFL renames its divisions "Eastern Conference" and "Western Conference."

Eastern Conference Winner: Cleveland (11-1-0). The Browns' only loss is to Philadelphia, 42-27, in their final game following 11 straight wins. Otto Graham is NFL's top-ranked quarterback with a 65% pass completion rate and 2,722 yds gained in the air. Halfback Ray Renfro and ends Dante Lavelli and Darrell Brewster are his top receivers. Walt Michaels, Tommy Thompson, Darrell Palmer and Len Ford lead the defense.

Western Conference Winner: [Note: The Baltimore Colts replace the Dallas Texans in the NFL Western Conference.] Detroit (10-2-0). The Lions repeat as NFL West champions, losing only to Los Angeles (twice). Quarterback Bobby Layne passes for over 2,000 yds and Doak Walker leads the club in receiving, kicking and scoring (93 points). Rookie linebacker Joe Schmidt sparks the defense.

League Leaders: *Passer:* Otto Graham (Cleveland); *Rusher:* Joe Perry (San Francisco); *Receiver:* Pete Pihos (Philadelphia); *Scorer:* Lou Groza (Cleveland).

COLLEGE BOWLS & PRO CHAMPIONSHIPS

College Bowl Games
ROSE BOWL:
   Michigan State 28, UCLA 20
SUGAR BOWL:
   Georgia Tech 42, West Virginia 19
COTTON BOWL:
   Rice 28, Alabama 6
As Rice's All-American halfback Dicky Moegle races down the sideline en route to a sure TD, Alabama fullback Tommy Lewis leaps off the bench and tackles Moegle as he streaks by. Rice is later awarded a TD.
ORANGE BOWL:
   Oklahoma 7, Maryland 0
Larry Grigg, Oklahoma halfback, scores the game's only TD as the Sooners upset top-ranked Maryland (which plays without its injured quarterback Bernie Faloney).

NFL
Championship Game: Detroit 17, Cleveland 16. Lou Groza's 3 field goals are not enough for the Browns, who lose their 3d straight championship game. The Lions hold Cleveland's star quarterback Otto Graham to 2 completions out of 15 attempts for 20 yds. Detroit wins with 2 minutes left when Bobby Layne hits end Jim Doran with a 33-yd TD pass. Cleveland fullback Chick Jagade gains 104 yds on the ground in a losing cause.

COLLEGE REGULAR SEASON

The Ivy League (Brown, Cornell, Columbia, Dartmouth, Harvard Pennsylvania, Princeton and Yale) adopts a new code of ethics that abolishes spring practice, most athletic scholarships and all postseason games.

Alan Ameche, Wisconsin's powerful fullback, captures the Heisman Trophy. Kurt Burris (Oklahoma) and Howard Cassady (Ohio State) are runners-up.

Frank Leahy retires as Notre Dame's head coach because of ill health. During his 11-year career, Notre Dame wins 87 games, loses 11 and ties 9. Leahy's successor, Terry Brennan, leads the Fighting Irish to a 9-1-0 record in his first year.

Oklahoma, with 10 straight wins (and 19 over 2 seasons), is #1 in the polls. Other teams in the top 10 include Ohio State, UCLA, Nebraska, Mississippi, Duke, Arkansas, Notre Dame, Navy and Georgia Tech.

Conference Champions
BIG TEN: Ohio State
BIG SEVEN: Oklahoma
SOUTHEASTERN: Mississippi
SOUTHWEST: Arkansas
MISSOURI VALLEY: Wichita
ATLANTIC COAST: Duke
SOUTHERN: West Virginia
PACIFIC COAST: UCLA

1954 All-American Team
E: Ron Beagle (Navy), Frank McDonald (Miami, Fla.)
T: Jack Ellena (UCLA), Rex Boggan (Mississippi)
G: Bud Brooks (Arkansas), Ralph Chesnauskas (Army)
C: Kurt Burris (Oklahoma)
B: Ralph Guglielmi (Notre Dame), Howard Cassady (Ohio State), Dicky Moegle (Rice), Alan Ameche (Wisconsin)

PROFESSIONAL REGULAR SEASON

NFL
Eastern Conference Winner: Cleveland (9-3-0). The Browns win their 6th conference title in a row. After losing 2 out of 3 games (including a 55-27 rout by Pittsburgh), Cleveland wins 8 of its 9 remaining games. Quarterback Otto Graham continues as the NFL's #1 passer with a 59% pass completion rate. Ends Dante Lavelli and Darrell Brewster snare 89 passes for 1,478 yds. The defense, led by Len Ford and Doug Atkins, holds all rivals to 1,050 yds rushing and 162 points, best in the NFL.

Western Conference Winner: Detroit (9-2-1). The Lions take their 3d straight conference title, led by quarterback Bobby Layne and Doak Walker's all-round performance (running, kicking and receiving). Defensive standouts are Jack Christiansen (8 interceptions), Joe Schmidt and Les Bingaman.

League Leaders: *Passer:* Bobby Layne (Detroit); *Rusher:* Joe Perry (San Francisco); *Receiver:* Harlon Hill (Chicago); *Scorer:* Bobby Walston (Philadelphia).

COLLEGE BOWLS & PRO CHAMPIONSHIPS

College Bowl Games
ROSE BOWL:
  Ohio State 20, USC 7
SUGAR BOWL:
  Navy 21, Mississippi 0
This marks the first appearance by Navy in a bowl game.
COTTON BOWL:
  Georgia Tech 14, Arkansas 6
ORANGE BOWL:
  Duke 34, Nebraska 7

NFL
Championship Game: Cleveland 56, Detroit 10. Quarterback Otto Graham puts on a one-man offensive performance, passing for 3 TDs and rushing for 3 more as the Browns win their first NFL championship game after 3 straight losses. The Lions lose 3 fumbles and quarterback Bobby Layne is intercepted 6 times in the most one-sided championship game since 1940. The Browns' defense holds Detroit scoreless in the 2d half, while the offense racks up 21 points to complete the rout.

1955

COLLEGE REGULAR SEASON

Edward Kennedy, youngest son of the famous Massachusetts family, scores Harvard's only TD in a 21-7 loss to Yale.

The College All-Stars upset the NFL champion Cleveland Browns, 30-27.

The U.S. Air Force Academy begins its first football season with a win by its freshman squad, 34-18, over the Denver University frosh.

Oklahoma, undefeated in 10 games (and winner of 29 straight over 3 seasons) ranks #1 in the polls for the second year in a row. Michigan State, Maryland (10-0-0), UCLA, Ohio State, Texas Christian, Georgia Tech, Auburn, Notre Dame and Mississippi round out the top 10.

Howard "Hopalong" Cassady of Ohio State wins the Heisman Trophy, finishing ahead of Jim Swink (Texas Christian) and George Welsh (Navy).

Conference Champions
BIG TEN: Ohio State
PACIFIC COAST: UCLA
BIG SEVEN: Oklahoma
IVY LEAGUE: Princeton
SOUTHERN: West Virginia
SOUTHEASTERN: Mississippi
SOUTHWEST: Texas Christian
MISSOURI VALLEY: Detroit & Wichita

1955 All-American Team
E: Ron Beagle (Navy), Howard Schnellenberger (Kentucky)
T: Paul Wiggin (Stanford), Frank D'Agostino (Auburn)
G: Jim Brown (UCLA), Pat Bisceglia (Notre Dame)
C: Bob Pellegrini (Maryland)
B: Earl Morrall (Michigan State), Howard Cassady (Ohio State), Tommy McDonald (Oklahoma), Jim Swink (Texas Christian)

PROFESSIONAL REGULAR SEASON

NFL
Eastern Conference Winner: Cleveland (9-2-1). The Browns win their 7th conference title in a row. Quarterback Otto Graham, in his final season before retirement, leads the NFL East with a 53% completion rate. Ray Renfro, Dante Lavelli and Darrell Brewster are his top receivers (18 TDs and 1,717 yds combined). The NFL's #1 defense holds its opponents to under 100 yds per game average and only 218 total points.

Western Conference Winner: Los Angeles (9-2-1). New coach Sid Gillman leads the Rams to their first conference title since 1951. Quarterback Norm Van Brocklin's passes to Tom Fears and "Crazy Legs" Hirsch net over 1,000 yds, while halfback Ron Waller and fullback Tank Younger rush for 1,360 yds. Will Sherman, Ed Hughes, Andy Robustelli and "Big Daddy" Lipscomb are defensive stars.

League Leaders: *Passer:* Otto Graham (Cleveland); *Rusher:* Alan Ameche (Baltimore); *Receiver:* Pete Pihos (Philadelphia); *Scorer:* Doak Walker (Detroit).

COLLEGE BOWLS & PRO CHAMPIONSHIPS

College Bowl Games
ROSE BOWL:
   Michigan State 17, UCLA 14
SUGAR BOWL:
   Georgia Tech 7, Pittsburgh 0
Pittsburgh's Bobby Grier is the first black player in Sugar Bowl history. A controversial pass interference called against him leads to the game's only score (Grier also makes a great catch of a pass and gets off a 26-yd run from scrimmage).
COTTON BOWL:
   Mississippi 14, Texas Christian 13
ORANGE BOWL:
   Oklahoma 20, Maryland 6
This is the 30th victory in a row for Oklahoma, while the loss is Maryland's first after 15 straight wins. Sooner defensive back Carl Dodd returns an interception 82 yds to clinch victory.

NFL
Championship Game: Cleveland 38, Los Angeles 14. The Browns repeat as NFL champions, jumping out to a 17-7 halftime lead on Don Paul's 65-yd runback of an intercepted pass and quarterback Otto Graham's 50-yd pass play to Dante Lavelli with 39 seconds left. Graham, playing his last game before retirement, scores twice on short runs in the 3d quarter to put the game out of reach for the Rams. Cleveland's defense intercepts 6 Norm Van Brocklin passes to stop the Rams' potent passing game.

COLLEGE REGULAR SEASON

Jim Brown, playing his last college game for Syracuse, scores 6 TDs and kicks 7 extra points against Brown to set a new major college record of 43 points in one game.

Oklahoma goes undefeated for the 3d year in a row, stretching its unbeaten string to 40 straight, an all-time record. Other top teams in 1956 are Iowa, Oregon State, Texas A&M, Tennessee, Clemson and Michigan State.

Paul Hornung, Notre Dame's All-American halfback, captures the Heisman Trophy, the 5th Notre Dame player to receive the award. Johnny Majors (Tennessee) and Tommy McDonald (Oklahoma) are runners-up.

Conference Champions

BIG TEN: Iowa
PACIFIC COAST: Oregon State
BIG SEVEN: Oklahoma
MISSOURI VALLEY: Houston
SOUTHWEST: Texas A&M
SOUTHERN: West Virginia
ATLANTIC COAST: Clemson
SOUTHESTERN: Tennessee

1956 All-American Team

E: Joe Walton (Pittsburgh), Ron Kramer (Michigan)
T: Alex Karras (Iowa), John Witte (Oregon State)
G: Bill Glass (Baylor), Jim Parker (Ohio State)
C: Jerry Tubbs (Oklahoma)
B: Tommy McDonald (Oklahoma), Johnny Majors (Tennessee), Jim Brown (Syracuse), Don Bosseler (Miami, Fla.)

PROFESSIONAL REGULAR SEASON

NFL

Eastern Conference Winner: New York (8-3-1). Defense is the Giants' strongpoint, featuring rookie linebacker Sam Huff and veterans Andy Robustelli, Em Tunnell and Jack Stroud. They limit the opposition to 1,443 yds rushing, best in the NFL. Quarterback Chuck Conerly and halfbacks Frank Gifford and Alex Webster lead the offense.

Western Conference Winner: Chicago (9-2-1). The Bears, under new coach Paddy Driscoll, win their first conference title since 1946. The defense, led by linebackers Bill George and Joe Fortunato, is the best in the NFL West. Quarterback Ed Brown is ranked #1 in NFL with a 67% pass completion rate (1,667 yds and 11 TDs passing). Fullback Rick Casares is the only NFL player with over 1,000 yds rushing.

League Leaders: *Passer:* Ed Brown (Chicago); *Rusher:* Rick Casares (Chicago); *Receiver:* Billy Howton (Green Bay); *Scorer:* Bobby Layne (Detroit).

COLLEGE BOWLS & PRO CHAMPIONSHIPS

College Bowl Games

ROSE BOWL:
Iowa 35, Oregon State 17
SUGAR BOWL:
Baylor 13, Tennessee 7
Tennessee's All-American back, Johnny Majors, fumbles a punt in the 4th quarter to set up a game-winning TD for Baylor. It was Tennessee's first and only loss of the season and marked the 4th time that an undefeated volunteer team had a perfect season ruined in a bowl game.
COTTON BOWL:
Texas Christian 28, Syracuse 27
ORANGE BOWL:
Colorado 27, Clemson 21

NFL

Championship Game: New York 47, Chicago 7. Wearing sneakers on a frozen field, the Giants score 34 points in the 2d half to put the game out of the Bears' reach. Quarterback Chuck Conerly throws 2 TD passes, Alex Webster rushes for 2 more, and Ben Agajanian kicks 2 field goals to lead the Giant offense. New York's defense stops Chicago's ground game (67 yds), intercepts 2 passes and scores a TD when Henry Moore falls on a blocked punt in the Bears' end zone.

COLLEGE REGULAR SEASON

Heavy underdog Notre Dame (4-2) ends Oklahoma's record 48-game unbeaten string, 7-0 (Nov. 16). Halfback Dick Lynch scores the game's only points in the 4th quarter to win. It also marks the first time Oklahoma has been held scoreless in the last 123 games.

John David Crow (Texas A&M) is the 1957 winner of the Heisman Trophy, beating out Alex Karras of Iowa and Walt Kowalczyk of Michigan State.

Auburn, completing its first perfect season since 1913, gives up only 4 TDs in 10 games to earn top ranking in the nation. Others in the top 10 include Ohio State, Michigan State, Oklahoma, Navy, Iowa, Mississippi, Rice, Texas A&M and Notre Dame.

Conference Champions

BIG TEN: Ohio State
SOUTHEASTERN: Auburn
BIG EIGHT: Oklahoma
MISSOURI VALLEY: Houston
SOUTHWEST: Rice
SOUTHERN: Virginia Military
ATLANTIC COAST: North Carolina State

1957 All-American Team

E: Jim Phillips (Auburn), Dick Wallen (UCLA)
T: Alex Karras (Iowa), Lou Michaels (Kentucky)
G: Aurelius Thomas (Ohio State), Bill Krisher (Oklahoma)
C: Dan Currie (Michigan State)
B: King Hill (Rice), Dick Christy (North Carolina State), Jim Pace (Michigan), John Crow (Texas A&M)

PROFESSIONAL REGULAR SEASON

NFL

Eastern Conference Winner: Cleveland (9-2-1). Jimmy Brown makes his debut in the Cleveland backfield and leads the league with 942 yds gained rushing and 9 TDs. He is the first rookie ever named Player of the Year in NFL history. Cleveland's defense leads the league against the pass and gives up the fewest points (172).

Western Conference Winner: Detroit (8-4-0). Coach Buddy Parker quits before the season opener and his assistant, George Wilson, takes over, leading the team to a conference title. The regular season ends with the Lions and San Francisco 49ers tied for the lead. Detroit wins the playoff game, 31-27. Bobby Layne and Tobin Rote share quarterback duties. Yale Lary, Joe Schmidt and Ray Krouse lead on defense.

League Leaders: *Passer:* Y.A. Tittle (San Francisco); *Rusher:* Jim Brown (Cleveland); *Receiver:* Ray Berry (Baltimore); *Scorer:* Lou Groza (Cleveland).

COLLEGE BOWLS & PRO CHAMPIONSHIPS

College Bowl Games

ROSE BOWL:
  Ohio State 10, Oregon 7
SUGAR BOWL:
  Mississippi 39, Texas 7
COTTON BOWL:
  Navy 20, Rice 7
ORANGE BOWL:
  Oklahoma 48, Duke 21

NFL

Championship Game: Detroit 59, Cleveland 14. The Lions take a 31-7 lead at half without star quarterback Bobby Layne, who is injured. His replacement, Tobin Rote, scores a TD along with halfback Gene Gedman, end Steve Junker and defensive back Terry Barry (19-yd return of a pass interception). In the 3d quarter, Rote completes a 78-yd pass play to Jim Doran and a 23-yarder to Junker. Rote, who completes 63% of his passes, throws his 4th TD pass in the final quarter for the 2d highest point total in NFL championship game history.

COLLEGE REGULAR SEASON

The NCAA sanctions the two-point conversion following a TD as an alternative to the kicked extra point.

Louisiana State, ranked #1 in the nation, is the only major college team to enjoy a perfect season, its first all-winning season in 50 years. Other top-rated teams include Iowa, Army, Auburn, Oklahoma, Air Force, Wisconsin, Ohio State, Syracuse and Texas Christian. Auburn runs its unbeaten streak to 24 games, and Oklahoma, winner of 72 consecutive Big Eight Conference games, captures its 11th conference title.

Pete Dawkins of Army is the 1958 Heisman Trophy winner. Randy Duncan of Iowa and Billy Cannon of Louisiana State finish 2d and 3d in the balloting.

Other Conference Champions
BIG TEN: Iowa
IVY LEAGUE: Dartmouth
SOUTHEASTERN: Louisiana State
ATLANTIC COAST: Clemson
SOUTHERN: West Virginia
SOUTHWEST: Texas Christian
PACIFIC COAST: California

1959 All-American Team
E: Jim Houston (Ohio State), Buddy Dial (Rice)
T: Ted Bates (Oregon State), Brock Strom (Air Force)
G: Zeke Smith (Auburn), George Diederich (Vanderbilt)
C: Bob Harrison (Oklahoma)
B: Randy Duncan (Iowa), Billy Cannon (Louisiana State), Bill Austin (Rutgers), Pete Dawkins (Army)

PROFESSIONAL REGULAR SEASON

NFL
Eastern Conference Winner: New York (9-3-0). Tied with Cleveland at the end of the regular season, the Giants win the playoff game, 10-0, for the conference title. Quarterback Chuck Conerly and a trio of running backs lead the offense. Defensive stars include San Huff, Em Tunnell, Andy Robustelli and Dick Modzelewski.

In Cleveland, Jim Brown breaks Steve Van Buren's rushing record for one season with 1,527 yds.
Western Conference Winner: Baltimore (9-3-0). Despite losing All-Pro quarterback Johnny Unitas for 3 games with broken ribs, the Colts edge out Chicago for the conference title. Alan Ameche and Lenny Moore gain 1,389 yds (conbined) on the ground. Baltimore's defense is the best in the NFL West, allowing only 1,291 yds total.

The Green Bay Packers finish last, winning only 1 game despite the presence of Bart Starr, Paul Hornung, Jim Taylor, Forrest Gregg, Jerry Kramer and other stars. At the end of the season, Vince Lombardi is named the new head coach of the Packers.
League Leaders: *Passer:* Billy Wade (Chicago); *Rusher:* Jim Brown (Cleveland); *Receiver:* Raymond Berry (Baltimore); *Scorer:* Jim Brown (Cleveland).

COLLEGE BOWLS & PRO CHAMPIONSHIPS

ROSE BOWL:
   Iowa 38, California 12
SUGAR BOWL:
   Louisiana State University 7, Clemson 0
COTTON BOWL:
   Texas Christian 0, Air Force 0
The Air Force team, which includes the academy's first senior class, compiles a record of 9-0-1, then holds TCU to a scoreless tie in its first bowl appearance.
ORANGE BOWL:
   Oklahoma 21, Syracuse 6

NFL
Championship Game: Baltimore 23, New York 17. The Colts take a 14-3 lead at the half on Alan Ameche's 2-yd plunge and Johnny Unitas's pass to Ray Berry. The Giants move ahead in the 2d half on Mel Triplett's 1-yd dive and Charley Conerly's TD pass to Frank Gifford. Baltimore ties the score with 7 seconds left on Steve Myhra's 20-yd field goal. In the first overtime period of a championship game since the sudden-death rule went into effect, Baltimore wins when Unitas hits Berry on a 35-yd pass play followed by Alan Ameche's plunge from the 1-yd line.

COLLEGE REGULAR SEASON

Syracuse, coached by Ben Schwartzwalder, is the only major college team to finish its season undefeated, with a record of 10-0-0, and is named the #1 team in the nation. It is also the first undefeated season in Syracuse football history.

Trailing undefeated Mississippi, 3-0, with only 10 minutes left to play, Billy Cannon of Louisiana State runs back a punt 89 yds for a TD to assure LSU of its 19th win in a row.

Navy pulls off a stunning upset over favored Army, 43-12, in their annual football classic played before 100,000 fans in Philadelphia. It is the highest score in 60 games played between the rival academies.

In another surprise, underdog Northwestern crushes mighty Oklahoma, 45-13. The Sooners had been named the nation's top team in preseason polls.

Billy Cannon of Louisiana State wins the Heisman Trophy. Richie Lucas (Penn State) and Don Meredith (Southern Methodist) are runners-up.

1959 All-American Team
E: Monty Stickles (Notre Dame), Bill Carpenter (Army)
T: Dan Lanphear (Wisconsin), Don Floyd (Texas Christian)
G: Roger Davis (Syracuse), Bill Burrell (Illinois)
C: Maxie Baughan (Georgia Tech)
B: Richie Lucas (Penn State), Billy Cannon (Louisiana State), Ron Burton (Northwestern), Charley Flowers (Mississippi)

PROFESSIONAL REGULAR SEASON

NFL
Eastern Conference Winner: New York (10-2-0). The Giants' quarterback Chuck Conerly, 35, leads the team to its second straight conference title with 14 TD passes and 1,706 yds passing. New York's defense, which features Sam Huff, Rosie Grier and Andy Robustelli, leads the NFL against both the run (1,261 yds) and pass (1,811 yds). During the game between the Philadelphia Eagles and Pittsburgh Steelers on Oct. 11, NFL commissioner Bert Bell collapses and dies of a heart attack.

Western Conference Winner: Baltimore (9-3-0). The Colts repeat their conference championship. Quarterback Johnny Unitas leads the NFL in TD passes (32) and yds gained passing (2,899). Fullback Alan Ameche is the top ground gainer. Defense is led by Dick Szymanski, "Big Daddy" Lipscomb and Gino Marchetti.

League Leaders: *Passer:* Johnny Unitas (Baltimore); *Rusher:* Jim Brown (Cleveland); *Receiver:* Raymond Berry (Baltimore); *Scorer:* Paul Hornung (Green Bay).

COLLEGE BOWLS & PRO CHAMPIONSHIPS

College Bowl Games
ROSE BOWL:
    Washington 44, Wisconsin 8
SUGAR BOWL:
    Mississippi 21, Louisiana State University 0
COTTON BOWL:
    Syracuse 23, Texas 14
In the opening minute of play, Gerhard Schwedes of Syracuse hits All-American teammate Ernie Davis with a 35-yd pass. Davis races 50 yds for a TD.
ORANGE BOWL:
    Georgia 14, Missouri 0
LIBERTY BOWL:
    Penn State 7, Alabama 0
In the first Liberty Bowl game, Bear Bryant, coach of Alabama, begins a streak of 24 consecutive bowl game appearances, ending in a return to the Liberty Bowl in 1982.

NFL
Championship Game: Baltimore 31, New York 16. Trailing 9-7 after 3 quarters, the Colts explode for 24 points in the 4th quarter to beat N.Y. for their 2d NFL crown in a row. Johnny Unitas's TD pass to Lenny Moore in the 1st quarter is offset by 3 consecutive field goals by Giant kicker Pat Summerall. Colt scores in the final quarter come on Unitas's quarterback sneak, a 12-yd pass (Unitas to Jerry Richardson), Johnny Sample's 42-yd runback of an interception and Steve Myhra's field goal.

Vince Lombardi, the coach who made Green Bay famous, at work on the Packer sidelines. Malcom W. Emmons

Few linebackers in professional football could match the strength and determination of **Sam Huff** who played 14 years as linebacker for the N.Y. Giants and the Washington Redskins. Malcom W. Emmons

Jim Brown of the Cleveland Browns on his way to another record-breaking performance. Malcom W. Emmons

Lenny Moore of the Baltimore Colts races for the goal line. Malcom W. Emmons

Baltimore's great quarterback, **Johnny Unitas,** uncorks another long pass completion. Malcom W. Emmons

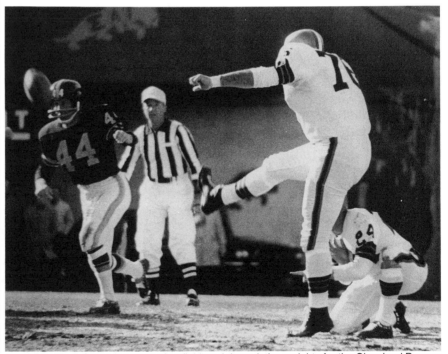

Lou "The Toe" Groza boots another field goal through the uprights for the Cleveland Browns. Malcom W. Emmons

COLLEGE REGULAR SEASON

The largest crowd of the season (98,616) watches Navy beat Army, 17-12, for its 9th win of the season (only loss is to Duke). Navy's Joe Bellino wins the Heisman Trophy.

Yale and New Mexico State are the nation's only major undefeated, untied teams (it is Yale's first perfect season since 1923).

Minnesota, coached by Murray Warmath, ties Iowa for the Big Ten crown and is named #1 team in the nation (despite an early loss to Purdue). Mississippi is ranked 2d.

Duke wins the Atlantic Coast championship, losing only to North Carolina in a major upset. Virginia Military Institute takes the Southern Conference crown.

Other Conference Champions
SOUTHWEST: Arkansas
SOUTHEASTERN: Mississippi
BIG FIVE: Washington
BIG EIGHT: Missouri
IVY LEAGUE: Yale

1960 All-American Team
E: Mike Ditka (Pittsburgh), Dan LaRose (Missouri)
T: Bob Lilly (Texas Christian), Ken Rice (Auburn)
G: Tom Brown (Minnesota), Joe Romig (Colorado)
C: E.J. Holub (Texas Tech)
B: Jake Gibbs (Mississippi), Joe Bellino (Navy), Ernie Davis (Syracuse), Bob Ferguson (Ohio State)

PROFESSIONAL REGULAR SEASON

NFL
Pete Rozelle, 33-year-old general manager of the Los Angeles Rams, is named new NFL commissioner, replacing Bert Bell. The Chicago Cardinal franchise is moved to St. Louis, and a new Dallas team is organized under coach Tom Landry.

Eastern Conference Winner: Chuck Bednarik, 35, of the Philadelphia Eagles, is the last man to play both offense (center) and defense (linebacker). He and teammate Norm Van Brocklin (quarterback), 34, lead the Eagles to a conference championship.

Western Conference Winner: Paul Hornung, former Notre Dame star, leads the Green Bay Packers, coached by Vince Lombardi, to their first title since 1944. Hornung sets a league record for most points scored in one season (176).

League Leaders: *Passer:* Milt Plum (Cleveland); *Rusher:* Jim Taylor (Green Bay); *Receiver:* Ray Berry (Baltimore); *Scorer:* Paul Hornung (Green Bay).

AFL
In its first year of existence, the American Football League (AFL) fields 8 teams in 2 conferences (Eastern and Western).

Eastern Conference Winner: Houston Oilers, led by halfback Billy Cannon and quarterback George Blanda, lead the division with a 10-4-0 record.

Western Conference Winner: Los Angeles Chargers, under coach Sid Gilman, win the conference title with a 10-4-0 record. Quarterback Jack Kemp leads the offense.

League Leaders: *Passer:* Frank Tripucka (Denver); *Rusher:* Abner Haynes (Dallas); *Receiver:* Bill Groman (Houston); *Scorer:* Gene Mingo (Denver).

COLLEGE BOWLS & PRO CHAMPIONSHIPS

College Bowl Games
ROSE BOWL:
Washington 17, Minnesota 7
SUGAR BOWL:
Mississippi 14, Rice 6
COTTON BOWL:
Duke 7, Arkansas 6
ORANGE BOWL:
Missouri 21, Navy 14

NFL
Championship Game: Philadelphia 17, Green Bay 13. Green Bay scores first on a Paul Hornung field goal following a fumble recovery on the first play from scrimmage. Hornung boots his 2d field goal early in the 2d quarter. Tommy McDonald, Eagles' flanker, snags a pass from quarterback Norm Van Brocklin. Bobby Walston kicks a field goal to put the Eagles in front at the half, 10-6.

Green Bay takes the lead, 13-10, in the 2d half on Bart Starr's pass to Max McGee. Eagles score the winning TD on a 5-yd run by Ted Dean.

AFL
Championship Game: Houston 24, Los Angeles 16. Ben Agajanian puts L.A. ahead with 2 quick field goals in the 1st quarter, then kicks another with 5 seconds left in the half. George Blanda puts Houston in front at the half, passing to Dave Smith for a TD and kicking a field goal. Blanda throws 2 more TD passes in the 2d half to clinch the championship for the Oilers.

COLLEGE REGULAR SEASON

Bill Cosby, halfback for the Temple Owls (and later to become a famous comedic actor), averages 3.5 yds per game on 36 rushing attempts.

Halfback Ernie Davis of Syracuse is the first black player to win the Heisman Trophy. Another black athlete, Bob Ferguson (Ohio State), finishes 2d in the balloting.

Alabama and Rutgers are the only major college teams to win all their games. Coach Bear Bryant's Crimson Tide holds its last 5 opponents scoreless and is named the #1 team in the nation.

The annual Army-Navy game draws college football's first $1 million gate (including TV rights). Navy wins, 13-7.

Conference Champions
ATLANTIC COAST: Duke
SOUTHERN: Citadel
SOUTHEASTERN: Alabama
BIG TEN: Ohio State
IVY LEAGUE: Columbia & Harvard
BIG EIGHT: Colorado
SOUTHWEST: Texas & Arkansas
SKYLINE: Utah State & Wyoming
BIG FIVE: UCLA

1961 All-American Team
E: Gary Collins (Maryland), Pat Richter (Wisconsin)
T: Merlin Olsen (Utah State), Billy Neighbors (Alabama)
G: Joe Romig (Colorado), Roy Winston (Louisiana State)
C: Alex Kroll (Rutgers)
B: Sandy Stephens (Minnesota), Ernie Davis (Syracuse), Jim Saxton (Texas), Bob Ferguson (Ohio State)

PROFESSIONAL REGULAR SEASON

NFL
Eastern Conference Winner: Recently acquired quarterback Y.A. Tittle guides the New York Giants to a conference title. Alex Webster's rushing and Del Shofner's receiving are key factors in the team's offense.
Western Conference Winner: Green Bay repeats as NFL West champions with an 11-3-0 record. Bart Starr's precision passing, Jim Taylor's running and Paul Hornung's all-round play (146 points scored) lead the way.
League Leaders: *Passer:* Milt Plum (Cleveland); *Rusher:* Jimmy Brown (Cleveland); *Receiver:* Tommy McDonald (Philadelphia); *Scorer:* Paul Hornung (Green Bay)

AFL
Eastern Conference Winner: Despite a poor start, the Houston Oilers repeat as AFL East champs. Veteran quarterback George Blanda tosses a record 36 TD passes, boots 16 field goals and makes 64 conversions.
Western Conference Winner: The San Diego Chargers (formerly Los Angeles) repeat as division champions, winning their first 11 games in a row. Good defense, plus an offense built around quarterback Jack Kemp (15 TD passes) and halfback Paul Lowe (9 TDs), are keys to San Diego's success.
League Leaders: *Passer:* George Blanda (Houston); *Rusher:* Billy Cannon (Houston); *Receiver:* Lionel Taylor (Denver); *Scorer:* Gino Cappelletti (Boston)

COLLEGE BOWLS & PRO CHAMPIONSHIPS

College Bowl Games
ROSE BOWL:
    Minnesota 21, UCLA 3
SUGAR BOWL:
    Alabama 10, Arkansas 3
COTTON BOWL:
    Texas 12, Mississippi 7
ORANGE BOWL:
    Louisiana State 25, Colorado 7

NFL
Championship Game: Green Bay 37, New York 0. Green Bay's frigid weather is a key factor in the Packers' drubbing of the Giants. Paul Hornung rushes for 89 yds and scores 19 points. Their defense holds New York to 6 first downs and only 31 yds rushing.

AFL
Championship Game: Houston 10, San Diego 3. The Oilers repeat as AFL champions. George Blanda kicks a 45-yd field goal in the first half and tosses a 35-yd TD pass to Billy Cannon in the 2d half for all Houston's scoring. Ten interceptions and 7 fumbles mark a loosely played game.

COLLEGE REGULAR SEASON

The Western Athletic Conference is established, comprising Arizona, Arizona State, Brigham Young, New Mexico, Utah and Wyoming.

Dartmouth, coached by Bob Blackman, has a perfect season (9-0-0) and wins the Ivy League.

Undefeated Southern California is named #1 college team. Wisconsin is runner-up.

Quarterback Roger Staubach leads Navy to a 34-14 victory over Army before the season's largest crowd (98,613).

Quarterback Terry Baker of Oregon State is the 1962 winner of the Heisman Trophy. He leads the nation in total offense (2,276 yds). Halfback Jerry Stovall of Louisiana State is 2d in balloting.

Other Conference Champions

ATLANTIC COAST: Duke
SOUTHEASTERN: Mississippi
SOUTHERN: Virginia Military
WESTERN (BIG TEN): Wisconsin
MISSOURI VALLEY: Tulsa
BIG EIGHT: Oklahoma
SOUTHWEST: Texas
BIG SIX: USC
WESTERN ATHLETIC: New Mexico

1962 All-American Team

E: Hal Bedsole (USC), Pat Richter (Wisconsin)
T: Bobby Bell (Minnesota), Jim Dunaway (Mississippi)
G: John Treadwell (Texas), Jack Cvercko (Northwestern)
C: Lee Roy Jordan (Alabama)
B: Terry Baker (Oregon State), Jerry Stovall (Louisiana State), Mel Renfro (Oregon), George Saimes (Michigan State)

PROFESSIONAL REGULAR SEASON

NFL

Eastern Conference Winner: At 35, New York Giant quarterback Y.A. Tittle sets a league record with 33 TD passes and leads the Giants to their 13th conference title. Sam Huff, Rosey Grier and Andy Robustelli are defensive stars.

Western Conference Winner: Jim Taylor (1,474 yds and 19 TDs) and Bart Starr (62% pass completion average) lead the Packers to their 3d consecutive conference title. In all, 11 Green Bay players are named to All-Pro teams.

League Leaders: *Passer:* Bart Starr (Green Bay); *Rusher:* Jim Taylor (Green Bay); *Receiver:* Bobby Mitchell (Washington); *Scorer:* Jim Taylor (Green Bay).

AFL

Eastern Conference Winner: The Houston Oilers capture their 3d straight AFL East title under new coach Pop Ivy with an 11- 3-0 record. Charley Tolar leads the rushing attack and quarterback George Blanda adds 27 TD passes and 2,810 yds to his passing records (plus 11 field goals and 48 extra points).

Western Conference Winner: The Dallas Texans under Hank Stram win their conference and set up an all-Texas playoff with Houston. Quarterback Len Dawson is acquired from the NFL and completes 29 TD passes. Abner Haynes rushes for 1,049 yds and 13 TDs.

League Leaders: *Passer:* Len Dawson (Kansas City); *Rusher:* Cookie Gilchrist (Buffalo); *Receiver:* Lionel Taylor (Denver); *Scorer:* Gene Mingo (Denver).

COLLEGE BOWLS & PRO CHAMPIONSHIPS

College Bowl Games

ROSE BOWL:
   Southern California 42, Wisconsin 37
SUGAR BOWL:
   Missouri 17, Arkansas 13
COTTON BOWL:
   Louisiana State 13, Texas 0
ORANGE BOWL:
   Alabama 17, Oklahoma 0

NFL

Championship Game: Green Bay 16, New York 7. Cold weather shuts down the passing attacks of Bart Starr (Green Bay) and Y.A. Tittle (N.Y.). Green Bay's Jim Taylor rushes 31 times for 85 yards to lead the rugged Packer offense. Jerry Kramer's field goal and Taylor's 7-yd run give Green Bay a 10-0 halftime lead. Kramer boots two more field goals in the 2d half to offset the Giants' lone score on a blocked punt in the 3d quarter.

AFL

Championship Game: Dallas 20, Houston 17. In a "Battle of Texans," Dallas runs up a 17-0 halftime lead, then is held scoreless in the 2d half. Led by quarterback George Blanda's TD pass and a 31-yd field goal, the Oilers tie the score in the 4th quarter to force the game into overtime. Neither team scores in the first overtime period, but Dallas completes a 25-yd field goal by Tommy Brooker in the 2d overtime to win pro football's longest game up to this time.

COLLEGE REGULAR SEASON

Coach Darrell Royal leads the Texas Longhorns to an undefeated season and #1 ranking (Navy is second). Texas also wins the Southwest Conference for the third straight year.

Quarterback Roger Staubach of Navy is awarded the Heisman Trophy (he is the only underclassman ever to win the honor). Billy Lothridge (Georgia Tech) and Sherman Lewis (Michigan State) are runners-up.

Dartmouth upsets Princeton, 22-21, to share the Ivy League title with Princeton.

Pete Gogolak of Cornell, U.S. football's first soccer-style kicker, boots the longest field goal of the year (50 yds) against Lehigh.

Other Conference Champions
WESTERN: Illinois
BIG EIGHT: Nebraska
MISSOURI VALLEY: Cincinnati & Wichita
SOUTHEASTERN: Mississippi
ATLANTIC COAST: North Carolina & North Carolina State
SOUTHERN: Virginia Tech
BIG SIX: Washington
WESTERN ATHLETIC: New Mexico

1963 All-American Team
E: Vern Burke (Oregon State), James Kelly (Notre Dame)
T: Scott Appleton (Texas), Carl Eller (Minnesota)
G: Bob Brown (Nebraska), Richard Redman (Washington)
C: Dick Butkus (Illinois)
B: Roger Staubach (Navy), Gale Sayers (Kansas), Sherman Lewis (Michigan), Jay Wilkinson (Duke)

PROFESIONAL REGULAR SEASON

NFL
Eastern Conference Winner: The N.Y. Giants are conference winners for the third straight year, capturing 9 of the last 10 games on their schedule. Veteran quarterback Y.A. Tittle, 36, completes 60% of passes attempted for 3,145 yds and 36 TDs.

Jim Brown, the Cleveland Browns' great running back, sets an NFL record of 1,863 yds for one season, averaging 6.4 yds per carry.
Western Conference Winner: Chicago wins its 10th conference title, allowing its opponents only 10 points per game.
League Leaders: *Passer:* Y.A. Tittle (New York); *Rusher:* Jim Brown (Cleveland); *Receiver:* Bobby Joe Conrad (St. Louis); *Scorer:* Don Chandler (New York).

AFL
Eastern Conference Winner: Boston wins its first conference title in a playoff with Buffalo. Quarterback Babe Parilli and place kicker Gino Cappelletti (22 field goals) lead Boston.
Western Conference Winner: The San Diego Chargers win their third conference championship in 4 years by one game over Al Davis's Oakland Raiders. Quarterbacks Tobin Rote and John Hadl pass for over 3,000 yds, while Paul Lowe and Keith Lincoln rush for 1,838 yds and 13 TDs.
League Leaders: *Passer:* Tobin Rote (San Diego); *Rusher:* Cookie Gilchrist (Buffalo); *Receiver:* Art Powell (Oakland); *Scorer:* Gino Cappelletti (Boston).

The Professional Football Hall of Fame opens at Canton, Ohio. The following men are inducted: Sammy Baugh, Bert Bell, Johnny Blood, Joe Carr, Dutch Clark, Red Grange, George Halas, Mel Hein, Pete Henry, Cal Hubbard, Curly Lambeau, Tim Mara, George Marshall, Bronko Nagurski, Ernie Nevers, Jim Thorpe.

COLLEGE BOWLS & PRO CHAMPIONSHIPS

College Bowl Games
ROSE BOWL:
Illinois 17, Washington 7
SUGAR BOWL:
Alabama 12, Mississippi 7
COTTON BOWL:
Texas 28, Navy 6
ORANGE BOWL:
Nebraska 13, Auburn 7

NFL
Championship Game: Chicago 14, New York 10. New York opens the scoring on a 14-yd pass from quarterback Y.A. Tittle to Frank Gifford. It is matched by Billy Wade's quarterback sneak. Don Chandler's field goal puts the Giants in front at halftime. Following another Chandler field goal in the 3d quarter, the Bears win it on another quarterback sneak by Wade.

AFL
Championship Game: San Diego 51, Boston 10. The Chargers make a mockery of the Patriot's vaunted defense, rushing for 218 yds and passing for another 305 (including 173 by Tobin Rote and 112 by John Hadl). Keith Lincoln runs 67 yds for a TD and catches a 25-yd pass from Hadl for another. Paul Lowe runs 58 yds from scrimmage for a Charger TD and Rote tosses 2 TD passes.

COLLEGE REGULAR SEASON

In Ara Parseghian's first year as head coach, Notre Dame, after winning only 2 games in 1963, comes within 95 seconds of its first undefeated season since 1949, losing its final game of the year to USC, 20-17. Quarterback John Huarte wins the Heisman Trophy, with Tulsa's Jerry Rhome (see below) runner-up.

Princeton finishes its first undefeated season since 1951 and wins the Ivy League title.

Jerry Rhome, Tulsa quarterback, sets 16 new offensive records, including (one season) total offensive yardage (3,128) and TD passes (32). His career passing yardage (5,472 yds) also sets a record.

Alabama (8-0) is voted the nation's #1 team and captures the Southeastern Conference despite an injury to star quarterback Joe Namath in mid-season.

Other Conference Champions
BIG TEN: Michigan
BIG EIGHT: Nebraska
MISSOURI VALLEY: Cincinnati
BIG EIGHT (PACIFIC COAST):
  Oregon State & USC
SOUTHWEST: Arkansas
WESTERN ATHLETIC: Utah &
  New Mexico

1964 All-American Team
E: Jack Snow (Notre Dame), Larry Elkins (Maryland)
T: Larry Kramer (Nebraska), Ralph Neely (Oklahoma)
G: Rich Redman (Washington), Tommy Nobis (Texas)
C: Dick Butkus (Illinois)
B: John Huarte (Notre Dame), Jerry Rhome (Tulsa), Gale Sayers (Kansas), Jim Grabowski (Illinois)

PROFESSIONAL REGULAR SEASON

NFL
Eastern Conference Winner: The Cleveland Browns win their first conference title since 1957. Quarterback Frank Ryan has another good year (25 TD passes and 2,404 yds passing). Cleveland's peerless running back Jim Brown again leads the NFL with 1,446 yds rushing (5.2 yds per carry).
Western Conference Winner: The Baltimore Colts take the NFL West with a 12-2-0 record. Quarterback Johnny Unitas passes for 2,824 yds and halfback Lenny Moore returns from a leg injury to register 20 TDs (a league record).
League Leaders: *Passer:* Bart Starr (Green Bay); *Rusher:* Jim Brown (Cleveland); *Receiver:* Johnny Morris (Chicago); *Scorer:* Lenny Moore (Baltimore).

AFL
Eastern Conference Winner: The Buffalo Bills win their first conference title, led by 250-lb fullback Cookie Gilchrist (980 yds rushing) and quarterbacks Jack Kemp and Daryl Lamonica (19 TD passes and 3,342 passing yardage combined). Kicker Pete Gogolak, former Hungarian soccer player, scores 102 points in his first pro season.
Western Conference Winner: Defending champion San Diego Chargers repeat as AFL West champions. Quarterbacks John Hadl and Tobin Rote combine for 27 TD tosses and more than 3,000 total yds passing.
League Leaders: *Passer:* Len Dawson (Kansas City); *Rusher:* Cookie Gilchrist (Buffalo); *Receiver:* Charley Hennigan (Houston); *Scorer:* Gino Cappelletti (Boston).

Hall of Fame Inductees
Jimmy Conzelman, Ed Healey, Clarke Hinkle, Mike Michalske, Art Rooney, George Trafton

COLLEGE BOWLS & PRO CHAMPIONSHIPS

College Bowl Games
ROSE BOWL:
  Michigan 34, Oregon State 7
SUGAR BOWL:
  Louisiana State 13, Syracuse 10
COTTON BOWL:
  Arkansas 10, Nebraska 7
ORANGE BOWL:
  Texas 21, Alabama 17

NFL
Championship Game: Cleveland 27, Baltimore 0. After a scoreless 1st half, Lou Groza scores underdog Cleveland's first points with a 43-yd field goal. Gary Collins then catches 3 Frank Ryan passes for TDs, including a 51-yd bomb, for the Browns' first NFL championship since 1955. Jim Brown is the game's leading rusher (114 yds).

AFL
Championship Game: Buffalo 20, San Diego 7. Defending champion San Diego draws first blood on a 26-yd pass play from Tobin Rote to Dave Kocourek. Buffalo goes ahead at the half on 2 Pete Gogolak field goals and Wray Carlton's TD. Only score in the 2d half is Jack Kemp's quarterback sneak for a TD. A rib injury to running back Keith Lincoln hurts the Charger offense. Cookie Gilchrist and Carlton rush for 192 yds for the victorious Bills.

1965

COLLEGE REGULAR SEASON

The Michigan State Spartans' defense (average weight: 244 lbs.) holds its opponents to 45.6 yds rushing per game (including 3 teams with minus yards rushing) as the team finishes the season undefeated (10-0), wins the Big Ten championship and is named the top college team in the U.S. It is the first Big Ten team to go undefeated in a 10-game season since 1905. After Michigan State loses to USC in the Rose Bowl, AP names Alabama #1.

Mike Garrett of USC wins the Heisman Trophy..

Other Conference Champions
BIG EIGHT: Nebraska
AAWU (PACIFIC COAST): UCLA
WESTERN ATHLETIC: Brigham Young
SOUTHEASTERN: Alabama
SOUTHERN: West Virginia
SOUTHWEST: Arkansas
MISSOURI VALLEY: Tulsa

1965 All-American Team
This is the first year since 1951-1952 that offensive and defensive teams are selected.
(O = Offense; D = Defense)
E: Howard Twilley (O-Tulsa), Freeman White (O-Nebraska), Aaron Brown (D-Minnesota), Charles Smith (D-Michigan State)
T: Glen Ray Hines (O-Arkansas), Sam Ball (O-Kentucky), Lloyd Phillips (D-Arkansas), Bill Yearby (D-Michigan)
G: Dick Arrington (O-Notre Dame), Doug Van Horn (O-Ohio University), George Patton (D-Georgia)
C: Paul Crane (O-Alabama)
LB: Tom Nobis (D-Texas), Carl McAdams (D-Oklahoma), Dwight Kelly (D-Ohio State)
B: Bob Griese (O-Purdue), Mike Garrett (O-USC), Donny Anderson (O-Texas Tech), Jim Grabowski (O-Illinois), Nick Rassas (D- Notre Dame), George Webster (D-Michigan State), John Roland (D- Missouri)

PROESSIONAL REGULAR SEASON

NFL
Eastern Conference Winner: The Cleveland Browns repeat as NFL East champs. Jimmy Brown leads the league in rushing for the 8th time in the last 9 years with 1,544 yds. Gary Collins snags 50 Frank Ryan passes for 884 yds and 10 TDs.
Western Conference Winner: Vince Lombardi's mighty Green Bay machine wins its third conference title in 5 years. Quarterback Bart Starr completes 56% of passes attempted for 2,055 yds. Jim Taylor and Paul Hornung rush for 1,033 yds. The defense holds opponents to 214 points, best in the NFL.
League Leaders: *Passer:* Rudy Bukich (Chicago); *Rusher:* Jimmy Brown (Cleveland); *Receiver:* Dave Parks (San Francisco); *Scorer:* Gale Sayers (Chicago).

AFL
Eastern Conference Winner: The Buffalo Bills repeat as AFL East champions. Pete Gogolak boots 28 field goals and quarterback Jack Kemp completes 179 passes for 2,368 yds. The Bills' defense is the best in the AFL, limiting their rivals to 5 TDs by rushing.
Western Conference Winner: San Diego cruises to its fifth conference win in 6 years. Paul Lowe rushes for 1,121 yds to set a new AFL record. Quarterback John Hadl tosses for 2,798 yds and 20 TDs. Lance Alworth is the league's top receiver with 14 TDs and 1,602 yds.
League Leaders: *Passer:* Len Dawson (Kansas City); *Rusher:* Paul Lowe (San Diego); *Receiver:* Lance Alworth (San Diego); *Scorer:* Gino Cappelletti (Boston).

Hall of Fame Inductees
Guy Chamberlin, Paddy Driscoll, Danny Fortmann, Otto Graham, Sid Luckman, Steve Van Buren, Bob Waterfield

COLLEGE BOWLS & PRO CHAMPIONSHIPS

College Bowl Games
ROSE BOWL:
   UCLA 14, Michigan 12
SUGAR BOWL:
   Missouri 20, Florida 18
Florida quarterback Steve Spurrier sets 5 offensive records in a losing cause.
COTTON BOWL:
   Louisiana State 14, Arkansas 7
ORANGE BOWL:
   Alabama 39, Nebraska 28

NFL
Championship Game: Green Bay 23, Cleveland 12. A muddy field holds Cleveland's Jim Brown to 50 yds rushing. Paul Hornung and Jim Taylor pile up 204 yds on the ground for the Packers. Cleveland is held scoreless in the 2d half as Green Bay clinches the victory on Hornung's 13-yd TD run and Don Chandler's 3d field goal.

AFL
Championship Game: Buffalo 23, San Diego 0. Buffalo repeats as AFL champions, shutting out the high-scoring Chargers (340 points scored during the season). The Bills lead at the half on an 18-yd pass play from Jack Kemp to Ernie Warlick, and a 74-yd punt return by Butch Byrd. Pete Gogolak's 3 field goals in the 2d half seal the victory for Buffalo.

COLLEGE REGULAR SEASON

Notre Dame and Michigan State, both undefeated, meet in the "Game of the Decade" and play to a 10-10 tie (Nov. 19). Notre Dame, led by the sophomore passing combo of Terry Hanratty to Jim Seymour, outscores the opposition, 362 to 38, as the defense yields only 3 TDs all year.

Quarterback Virgil Carter of Brigham Young sets a record for total offense in a single game, piling up 599 yds (513 passing, 86 rushing) against Texas-El Paso.

Quarterback Steve Spurrier of Florida wins the Heisman Trophy. Bob Griese of Purdue is runner-up.

Conference Champions

BIG TEN: Michigan
BIG EIGHT: Nebraska
AAWU (PACIFIC COAST): USC
IVY LEAGUE: Harvard, Dartmouth & Princeton (3-way tie)
SOUTHEASTERN: Georgia & Alabama
SOUTHERN: William & Mary & East Carolina
SOUTHWEST: Southern Methodist

1966 All-American Team

(O = Offense; D = Defense)
E: Gene Washington (O-Michigan State), Jack Clancy (O- Michigan), Bubba Smith (D-Michigan State), Tom Greenlee (D- Washington)
T: Cecil Dowdy (O-Alabama), Ron Yary (O-USC), Lloyd Phillips (D-Arkansas), Pete Duranko (D-Notre Dame)
G: Tom Regner (O-Notre Dame), LaVerne Allers (O-Nebraska), Wayne Meylan (D-Nebraska)
C: Jim Breland (O-Georgia Tech)
LB: Jim Lynch (D-Notre Dame), Paul Naumoff (D-Tennessee)
B: Steve Spurrier (O-Florida), Nick Eddy (O-Notre Dame), Mel Farr (O-UCLA), Floyd Little (O-Syracuse), George Webster (D- Michigan State), Nate Shaw (D-USC), Tom Beier (D-Miami, Fla.), Martin Bercher (D-Arkansas)

PROFESSIONAL REGULAR SEASON

The AFL and NFL agree to merge in 1970. The champions of each league meet in an annual Super Bowl starting in January 1967.

NFL

Eastern Conference Winner: The Atlanta Falcons join the NFL East in 1966 and compile a 3-11-0 record.

The Dallas Cowboys, longtime NFL also-rans, win their first conference crown under coach Tom Landry. Quarterback Don Meredith leads the offense with 24 TD passes and 2,805 yds passing. Speedster Bob Hayes grabs 64 passes for 13 TDs.

Western Conference Winner: Green Bay repeats as NFL West winners, their 4th title in 6 years. Bart Starr completes 62% of passes attempted. Flanker Carroll Dale snags 37 passes for 876 yds and 7 TDs.

League Leaders: *Passer:* Bart Starr (Green Bay); *Rusher:* Gale Sayers (Chicago); *Receiver:* Pat Studstill (Detroit); *Scorer:* Bruce Gossett (Los Angeles).

AFL

Eastern Conference Winner: The Buffalo Bills win their 3d straight conference title. The Bills' defense holds its rivals to less than 80 yds per game. Quarterback Jack Kemp completes only 43% of passes, but a solid running game scores 19 TDs and gains 135 yds per game.

Western Conference Winner: The Kansas City Chiefs capture their first conference crown with an 11-2-1 record. Len Dawson is the AFL's leading passer with 28 TD tosses.

League Leaders: *Passer:* Len Dawson (Kansas City); *Rusher:* Jim Nance (Boston); *Receiver:* Lance Alworth (San Diego); *Scorer:* Gino Cappelletti (Boston).

Hall of Fame Inductees:

Bill Dudley, Joe Guyon, Arnie Herber, Walt Kiesling, George McAfee, Steve Owen, Shorty Ray

COLLEGE BOWLS & PRO CHAMPIONSHIPS

College Bowl Games

ROSE BOWL:
Purdue 14, USC 13
SUGAR BOWL:
Alabama 34, Nebraska 7
COTTON BOWL:
Georgia 24, Southern Methodist 9
ORANGE BOWL:
Florida 27, Georgia Tech 12

NFL

Championship Game: Green Bay 34, Dallas 27. The Packers win their 2d NFL championship in a row and 4th in the last 6 years. Bart Starr passes for 304 yds and 4 TDs to lead Green Bay.

AFL

Championship Game: Kansas City 31, Buffalo 7. Kansas City earns the right to play in Super Bowl I, holding the Bills to 40 yds on the ground and only 9 1st downs. Quarterback Len Dawson passes for 2 TDs and Mike Garrett rushes for 2 more to lead the Chiefs.

Super Bowl I

Green Bay 35, Kansas City 10. In a historic first encounter, the more experienced and talented Packers defeat the young Chiefs convincingly, rolling up 358 yds and holding Kansas City to 72 yds rushing. Quarterback Bart Starr's 37-yd pass play to Max McGee starts the scoring, but K.C. ties the score on Len Dawson's toss to Curtis McClinton. Green Bay goes ahead to stay on Jim Taylor's 14-yd run. The 2d half is all in the Packers' favor as Elijah Pitts runs for 2 TDs and McGee snares another Starr pass.

1967

COLLEGE REGULAR SEASON

All-American halfback O.J. Simpson leads USC to a national championship, rushing for 1,415 yds.

Quarterback Gary Beban (UCLA) is awarded the Heisman Trophy (Simpson is 2d in the balloting).

Quarterback Billy Stevens of Texas-El Paso sets 4 college passing records for one season: most TD passes (51); most yds gained passing (6,495); most passes attempted (943); most total offensive plays (1,091).

Conference Champions
SOUTHEASTERN: Tennessee
BIG TEN: Indiana, Purdue & Minnesota (3-way tie)
BIG EIGHT: Oklahoma
AAWU (PACIFIC COAST): USC
WESTERN ATHLETIC: Wyoming (only major college team with a perfect record in 1967)
IVY LEAGUE: Yale
ATLANTIC COAST: Clemson
SOUTHERN: West Virginia
SOUTHWEST: Texas
MISSOURI VALLEY: North Texas State

1967 All-American Team
(O = Offense; D = Defense)
E: Jim Seymour (O-Notre Dame), Dennis Homan (O-Arkansas), Ted Hendricks (D-Miami, Fla.), Tim Rossovich (D-USC)
T: Ron Yary (O-USC), Edgar Chandler (O-Georgia), Kevin Hardy (D-Notre Dame), Dennis Byrd (D-North Carolina State)
G: Rich Stotter (O-Houston), Harry Olszewski (O-Clemson), Granville Liggins (D-Oklahoma)
C: Bob Johnson (O-Tennessee)
LB: Adrian Young (D-USC), Don Manning (D-UCLA)
B: Gary Beban (O-UCLA), O.J. Simpson (O-USC), Leroy Keyes (O-Purdue), Larry Csonka (O-Syracuse), Tom Schoen (D-Notre Dame), Bobby Johns (D-Alabama), Frank Loria (D-Virginia Tech), Al Dorsey (D- Tennessee)

PROFESSIONAL REGULAR SEASON

NFL
Starting in 1967, the NFL is split into 4 divisions: Capitol and Central (Eastern Conference) and Central and Coastal (Western Conference).
Capitol Division Winner: Dallas (9-5-0)
Century Division Winner: Cleveland (9-5-0)
Central Division Winner: Green Bay (9-4-1)
Coastal Division Winner: Los Angeles (11-1-2)
League Leaders: *Passer:* Sonny Jurgenson (Washington); *Rusher:* Leroy Kelly (Cleveland); *Receiver:* Charley Taylor (Washington); *Scorer:* Jim Bakken (St. Louis).

AFL
Eastern Division Winner: Houston wins its first divisional title since 1962. The Oilers' defense is best in the league. Fullback Hoyle Granger gains over 1,000 yds to lead the offense.
Western Division Winner: Oakland loses only one game as new quarterback Daryle Lamonica leads the AFL with 30 TD passes and 3,225 yds passing.
League Leaders: *Passer:* Daryle Lamonica (Oakland); *Rusher:* Jim Nance (Boston); *Receiver:* Don Maynard (New York); *Scorer:* George Blanda (Houston).

Hall of Fame Inductees
Chuck Bednarik, Charles Bidwell, Paul Brown, Bobby Lane, Dan Reeves, Ken Strong, Joe Stydahar, Em Tunnell

COLLEGE BOWLS & PRO CHAMPIONSHIPS

College Bowl Games
ROSE BOWL:
USC 14, Indiana 3
SUGAR BOWL:
Louisiana State 20, Wyoming 13
COTTON BOWL:
Texas A&M 20, Alabama 16
ORANGE BOWL:
Oklahoma 26, Tennessee 24

NFL
Playoffs: East: Green Bay 28, Los Angeles 7; **West:** Dallas 52, Cleveland 14.
Championship Game: Green Bay 21, Dallas 17. After Bart Starr puts Green Bay ahead with 2 TD passes, Dallas converts 2 Green Bay fumbles into 10 points to trail 14-10 at halftime. Playing in sub-zero weather, Dallas goes ahead in the 4th quarter on a 50-yd pass play. With 20 seconds left, Starr sneaks over from the 1-yd line for the winning TD.

AFL
Championship Game: Oakland 40, Houston 7. Hewritt Dixon and Pete Banaszak rush for 260 yds to lead an Oakland rout over the Oilers, who gain only 38 yds on the ground.

Super Bowl II
Green Bay 33, Oakland 14. In Vince Lombardi's last game as head coach of the Packers, Don Chandler boots 3 field goals and Boyd Dowler scores on an 82-yd pass play from quarterback Bart Starr to give Green Bay a big lead. Only a Daryle Lamonica TD toss to Bill Miller keeps the Raiders in the game (16-7) at halftime. Chandler kicks his 4th field goal in the 3d quarter and Donny Anderson scores from 2 yds out to put the game on ice for Green Bay.

COLLEGE REGULAR SEASON

Traditional rivals Yale and Harvard both enter their annual clash undefeated for the first time since 1909. The game ends in a tie, 29-29, after Harvard overcomes a 29-13 deficit with only 42 seconds left.

Houston scores 76 points in the 4th quarter to rout Tulsa, 100-6, in one of the most lopsided games in college football history.

Ohio State (9-0) is named #1 in the nation for the 4th time. USC loses its bid for top ranking when it is tied by Notre Dame, 21-21, in the last game of the season. Trojan halfback O.J. Simpson wins the Heisman Trophy after scoring 22 TDs and setting a record for rushing in a single season.

Conference Champions
BIG TEN: Ohio State
BIG EIGHT: Oklahoma & Kansas
PACIFIC EIGHT: USC
SOUTHEASTERN: Georgia
ATLANTIC COAST: N.C. State
SOUTHWEST: Texas
MISSOURI VALLEY: Memphis State
IVY LEAGUE: Yale & Harvard

1968 All-American Team
(O = Offense; D = Defense)
E: Jim Seymour (O-Notre Dame), Ted Kwalik (O-Penn State), Ted Hendricks (D-Miami, Fla.), Joe Greene (D-Kansas)
T: Dave Foley (O-Ohio State), George Kunz (O-Notre Dame), Bill Stanfill (D-Georgia), Joe Greene (D-North Texas State)
G: Charle Rosenfelder (O-Tennessee), Guy Dennis (O- Florida), Chuck Kyle (D-Purdue)
C: John Didion (O-Oregon State)
LB: Dennis Onkotz (D-Penn State), Bill Hobbs (D-Texas A&M)
B: Terry Hanratty (O-Notre Dame), O.J. Simpson (O-USC), Leroy Keyes (O-Purdue), Bill Enyart (O-Oregon State), Roger Wehrli (D-Missouri), Mike Battle (D-USC), Jake Scott (D-Georgia), Al Worley (D-Washington)

PROFESSIONAL REGULAR SEASON

NFL
Eastern Conference:
Capitol Division Winner: Dallas (12-2-0)
Century Division Winner: Cleveland (10-4-0)
Western Conference:
Central Division Winner: Minnesota (8-6-0)
Coastal Division Winner: Baltimore (13-1-0)
League Leaders: *Passer:* Earl Morrall (Baltimore); *Rusher:* Leroy Kelly (Cleveland); *Receiver:* Clifton McNeil (San Francisco); *Scorer:* Leroy Kelly (Cleveland).

AFL
Eastern Division Winner:
The New York Jets come into their own behind brilliant quarterback Joe Namath (3,147 yds passing), receiver Don Maynard, and a solid but underrated defense.
Western Division Winner: The Oakland Raiders repeat as division champions despite a rash of injuries to key players. Quarterback Daryle Lamonica tosses 25 TD passes. George Blanda, now 40, boots 21 field goals and all 54 extra points attempted.
League Leaders: *Passer:* Len Dawson (Kansas City); *Rusher:* Paul Robinson (Cincinnati); *Receiver:* Lance Alworth (San Diego); *Scorer:* Jim Turner (New York).

Hall of Fame Inductees
Cliff Battles, Art Donovan, "Crazy Legs" Hirsch, Wayne Millner, Marion Motley, Charlie Trippi, Alex Wojciechowicz

COLLEGE BOWLS & PRO CHAMPIONSHIPS

College Bowl Games
ROSE BOWL:
Ohio State 27, USC 16
SUGAR BOWL:
Arkansas 16, Georgia 2
COTTON BOWL:
Texas 36, Tennessee 13
ORANGE BOWL:
Penn State 15, Kansas 14

First annual Peach Bowl is played Dec. 30. Louisiana State defeats Florida State, 31-27, in Atlanta.

NFL
Eastern Conference Playoffs: Cleveland 31, Dallas 20. Interceptions (4), Leroy Kelly's running and Bill Nelsen's passing are keys to Browns' victory.
Western Conference Playoffs: Baltimore 24, Minnesota 14. The Vikings' quarterback Joe Kapp completes 26 passes for 287 yds, but Baltimore wins on 2 Earl Morrall TD passes and a 60-yd fumble return by Mike Curtis.
Championship Game: Baltimore 34, Cleveland 0. Baltimore holds Leroy Kelly to 28 yds rushing and limits Earl Morrall to only 11 completed passes. Tom Matte (3 TDs) and Gerry Hill rush for 148 yds to lead the Colts' offense.

AFL
Championship Game: New York 27, Oakland 23. Despite Daryle Lamonica's 401-yd passing performance for Oakland, Joe Namath and his young Jets make it to Super Bowl III.

Super Bowl III
New York 16, Baltimore 7. The AFL comes into its own as New York stages the biggest upset in pro football history to date. Jim Turner boots 3 field goals and halfback Matt Snell rushes for 121 yds and the game's only TD.

1969

COLLEGE REGULAR SEASON

Unbeaten and top-ranked Ohio State is upset by Michigan in the last game of the regular season, 24-12, before a record crowd of 103,588 at Ann Arbor (Mich.). The Wolverines tie the Buckeyes for the Big Ten Conference title and win a trip to the Rose Bowl.

Texas, also undefeated, is named the top college team by the Associated Press. Penn State is ranked 2d, followed by USC, Ohio State, Notre Dame, Missouri, Arkansas, Mississippi, Michigan and Louisiana State.

Halfback Steve Owens of Oklahoma sets 8 NCAA rushing records and is awarded the Heisman Trophy. Mike Phipps, Purdue quarterback, is the runner-up.

Conference Champions
BIG TEN: Michigan & Ohio State
PACIFIC EIGHT: USC
BIG EIGHT: Missouri & Nebraska
SOUTHEASTERN CONFERENCE:
  Tennessee & Louisiana State
SOUTHWEST CONFERENCE:
  Texas
IVY LEAGUE: Dartmouth, Princeton, Yale (3-way tie)

1969 All-American Team
(O = Offense; D = Defense)
E: Carlos Alvarez (O-Florida), Jim Mandich (O-Michigan), Jim Gunn (D-USC), Phil Olsen (D-Utah State)
T: Sid Smith (O-USC), Bob McKay (O-Texas), Mike McCoy (D- Notre Dame), Mike Reid (D-Penn State)
G: Chip Kell (O-Tennessee), Larry DiNardo (O-Notre Dame), Jim Stillwagon (D-Ohio State)
C: Rodney Brand (O-Arkansas)
LB: Steve Kiner (D-Tennessee), Dennis Onkotz (D-Penn State)
B: Mike Phipps (O-Purdue), Steve Owens (O-Oklahoma), Jim Otis (O-Ohio State), Bob Anderson (O-Colorado), Glenn Cannon (D-Mississippi), Steve Curtis (D-Michigan), Neal Smith (D-Penn State), Buddy McClinton (D-Auburn)

PROFESSIONAL REGULAR SEASON

NFL
Eastern Conference:
Capitol Division Winner: Dallas (11-2-1). Calvin Hill is the Cowboys' leading rusher. Craig Morton's passes to Bob Hayes and Lance Rentzel produce 16 TDs.

Century Division Winner: Cleveland (10-3-1). Leroy Kelly and Ron Johnson rush for 16 TDs. Paul Warfield and Gary Collins snare 96 passes for 21 TDs.
Western Conference:
Central Division Winner: Minnesota (12-2-0). Quarterback Joe Kapp's erratic passes somehow find their marks. A strong Viking defense is key to success.
Coastal Division Winner: Los Angeles (11-3-0). A strong, veteran defensive line and quarterback Roman Gabriel's 24 TD passes spark the Rams.
League Leaders: *Passer:* Sonny Jurgensen (Washington); *Rusher:* Gayle Sayers (Chicago); *Receiver:* Lance Rentzel (Dallas); *Scorer:* Fred Cox (Minnesota).

AFL
Eastern Division Winner: The N.Y. Jets repeat as division winners over Houston by 2 games. Quarterback Joe Namath and running backs Emerson Boozer and Matt Snell provide a potent offense.
Western Division Winner: The Oakland Raiders take their division for the 3d year in a row, losing only to Cincinnati. Quarterback Daryle Lamonica wins the AFL's MVP award with 34 TD tosses and 221 completions.
League Leaders: *Passer:* Daryle Lamonica (Oakland); *Rusher:* Carl Garrett (Boston); *Receiver:* Warren Wells (Oakland); *Scorer:* Jim Turner (New York).

Hall of Fame Inductees
Turk Edwards, Greasy Neale, Leo Nomellini, Joe Perry, Ernie Stautner

COLLEGE BOWLS & PRO CHAMPIONSHIPS

College Bowl Games
ROSE BOWL:
  USC 10, Michigan 3
SUGAR BOWL:
  Mississippi 27, Arkansas 22
COTTON BOWL:
  Texas 21. Notre Dame 17
This is Notre Dame's first bowl game, ending a 44-year school ban on postseason play.
ORANGE BOWL:
  Penn State 10, Missouri 3

NFL
Eastern Conference Playoffs:
Minnesota 23, Los Angeles 20.
Western Conference Playoffs:
Cleveland 38, Dallas 14.
Championship Game: Minnesota 27, Cleveland 7. Cold weather helps the favored Vikings gain 222 yds rushing. Quarterback Joe Kapp runs for a TD and hits receiver Gene Washington on a 75- yard pass play in the 1st quarter.

AFL
Championship Game: Kansas City 17, Oakland 7. Having upset the 1969 Super Bowl champion Jets in a playoff, the Chiefs (who finished behind Oakland in the regular season) win a trip to Super Bowl IV. After tying the score 7-7 at halftime, Kansas City scores 10 points in the 2d half while holding the Raiders scoreless.

Super Bowl IV
Kansas City 23, Minnesota 7. Quarterback Len Dawson returns from a knee injury to lead the Chiefs to the AFL's second straight Super Bowl upset. Four Kansas City runners grind out 151 yds on the ground, while the defense limits Minnesota to only 67 yds rushing.

Paul Hornung of Green Bay takes a handoff from quarterback Bart Starr and slashes his way toward the end zone.
Malcom W. Emmons

Gale Sayers of the Chicago Bears is about to break loose for another of his long TD jaunts. Malcom W. Emmons

Y.A. Tittle of the New York Giants fakes a handoff and drops back to pass.
Malcom W. Emmons

Green Bay's all-pro quarterback, Bart Starr, pivots away from center for a quick handoff.
Malcom W. Emmons

"Broadway Joe" Namath, hero of Super Bowl III, gets set to heave another long bomb for the N.Y. Jets. Malcom W. Emmons

George Blanda, who played in the NFL for 27 years, boots still another field goal for the Oakland Raiders. Malcom W. Emmons

1970

COLLEGE REGULAR SEASON

Nebraska (10-0-1) wins its first national championship, with Notre Dame ranked #2.

Dartmouth, Arizona State and Toledo are the only major college teams with perfect records.

Jim Plunkett, Stanford quarterback, wins the Heisman Trophy (Joe Theismann of Notre Dame and Archie Manning of Mississippi are runners-up). Plunkett sets career records for most yds gained passing (7,544), most yds gained rushing and passing (7,887) and total offense (254.4 yds per game average).

USC ruins Notre Dame's perfect season for the 3d year in a row, beating the Fighting Irish, 38-28, in the last game of the season.

Conference Champions

BIG TEN: Ohio State
BIG EIGHT: Nebraska
PACIFIC EIGHT: Stanford
SOUTHWEST: Texas
MISSOURI VALLEY: Louisville
IVY LEAGUE: Dartmouth
SOUTHEASTERN: Louisiana State
ATLANTIC COAST: Wake Forest
SOUTHERN: William & Mary

1970 All-American Team

(O = Offense; D = Defense)
E: Tom Gatewood (O-Notre Dame), Ernie Jennings (O-Air Force), Bill Atessis (D-Texas), Charlie Weaver (D-Texas Christian)
T: Dan Dierdorf (O-Michigan), Bob Wuensch (O-Texas), Rock Perdom (D-Georgia Tech), Joe Ehrmann (D-Syracuse)
G: Chip Kell (O-Tennessee), Larry DiNardo (O-Notre Dame), Jim Stillwagon (D-Ohio State)
C: Don Popplewell (O-Colorado)
B: Jim Plunkett (O-Stanford), Steve Worster (O-Texas), John Brockington (O-Ohio State), Ed Marinaro (O-Cornell), Larry Willingham (D-Auburn), Clarence Ellis (D-Notre Dame), Mike Sensibaugh (D-Ohio State), Bill McClard (D-Arkansas)

PROFESSIONAL REGULAR SEASON

Now called the National Football Conference (NFC), the old NFL consists of 3 divisions: Eastern, Central and Western. Winners of each division, plus a "wild card" team, meet in postseason playoffs to decide who plays in the championship game and the Super Bowl.

NFL

Playoffs: Eastern Division winner, Dallas (10-4-0) vs. Central Division runner-up (Wild Card), Detroit (10-4-0); Dallas 5, Detroit 0. Central Division winner, Minnesota (12-2-0) vs. Western Division winner, San Francisco (10-3-1); San Francisco 17, Minnesota 14.
League Leaders: *Passer:* John Brodie (San Francisco); *Rusher:* Duane Thomas (Dallas); *Receiver:* Dick Gordon (Chicago); *Scorer:* Fred Cox (Minnesota).
The AFL becomes the 3-division American Football Conference (AFC) consisting of the original 10 teams plus Baltimore, Cleveland and Pittsburgh from the NFL. The playoff system is the same as the rival NFC.

AFC

Playoffs: Western Division winner, Oakland (8-4-2) vs. Eastern Division runner-up (Wild Card), Miami (10-4-0); Oakland 21, Miami 14. Eastern Division winner, Baltimore (11-2-1) vs. Central Division winner, Cincinnati (8-6-0); Baltimore 17, Cincinnati 6.
League Leaders: *Passer:* Daryle Lamonica (Oakland); *Rusher:* Floyd Little (Denver); *Receiver:* Marlin Briscoe (Buffalo); *Scorer:* Jan Stenerud (Kansas City).

Hall of Fame Inductees

Jack Christiansen, Tom Fears, Hugh McElhenney, Pete Pihos

COLLEGE BOWLS & PRO CHAMPIONSHIPS

College Bowl Games

ROSE BOWL:
   Stanford 27, Ohio State 17
SUGAR BOWL:
   Tennessee 34, Air Force 13
COTTON BOWL:
   Notre Dame 24, Texas 11
ORANGE BOWL:
   Nebraska 17, Louisiana State 12

NFC

Championship Game: Dallas 17, San Francisco 10. Cowboy running backs, rookie Duane Thomas and Walt Garrison, rush for 214 yds and 2 TDs to assure the Dallas win.

AFC

Championship Game: Baltimore 27, Oakland 17. George Blanda, 43, duels Johnny Unitas, 37, in a battle of veteran quarterbacks. A 68-yd pass play in the 4th quarter, Unitas to Ray Perkins, clinches the Colt victory.

Super Bowl V

Baltimore 16, Dallas 13. Jim O'Brien's 32-yd field goal with 5 seconds left wins for Baltimore in a game marred by 11 turnovers and 14 penalties. Chuck Howley, Dallas linebacker, is named MVP.

COLLEGE REGULAR SEASON

Nebraska, one of only two major college teams with perfect records, is named best in the country.

Toledo, also with a perfect record (12-0-0), wins its 35th in a row, the longest winning streak in college football.

Quarterback Pat Sullivan of Auburn wins the Heisman Trophy. Ed Marinaro (Cornell) and Greg Pruitt (Oklahoma) finish 2d and 3d in the balloting.

Conference Champions
BIG TEN: Michigan
BIG EIGHT: Nebraska
SOUTHWEST: Texas
PACIFIC EIGHT: Stanford
WESTERN ATHLETIC: Arizona State
ATLANTIC COAST: North Carolina
SOUTHERN: Richmond
SOUTHEASTERN: Alabama
IVY LEAGUE: Dartmouth & Cornell

1971 All-American Team
(O = Offense; D = Defense)
E: Johnny Rodgers (O-Nebraska), Terry Beasley (O-Auburn), Walt Patulski (D-Notre Dame), Willy Harper (D-Nebraska)
T: Jerry Sizemore (O-Texas), Dave Jayner (O-Penn State), Larry Jacobson (D-Nebraska), Mel Long (D-Toledo)
G: Royce Smith (O-Georgia), Reggie McKenzie (O-Michigan), Rich Glover (D-Nebraska)
C: Tom DeLeone (O-Ohio State)
LB: Mike Taylor (D-Michigan), Jackie Walker (D-Tennessee), Jeff Siemon (D-Stanford)
B: Pat Sullivan (O-Auburn), Ed Marinaro (O-Cornell), Greg Pruitt (O-Oklahoma), Johnny Musso (O-Alabama), Tommy Casanova (D-Louisiana State), Clarence Ellis (D-Notre Dame), Brad Van Pelt (D-Michigan State), Bobby Majors (D-Tennessee)

PROFESSIONAL REGULAR SEASON

NFC
Eastern Division Winner: Dallas (11-3-0). Roger Staubach takes over as fulltime quarterback and leads the Cowboys to the playoffs.
Central Division Winner: Minnesota (11-3-0). Defense continues to carry the load for coach Bud Grant.
Western Division Winner: San Francisco (9-5-0). Vic Washington and Ken Willard grind out 1,666 yds rushing to lead the 49ers.
League Leaders: *Passer:* Roger Staubach (Dallas); *Rusher:* John Brockington (Green Bay); *Receiver:* Bob Hayes (Dallas); *Scorer:* Curt Knight (Washington).

AFC
Eastern Division Winner: Miami (10-3-1). Dolphins win the title in the final week of the season over Baltimore. Bob Griese's passing and the best running game in the AFC (2,429 yds) are key factors.
Central Division Winner: Cleveland (9-5-0). Despite a mediocre offense, the Browns make it safely into the playoffs.
Western Division Winner: Kansas City (10-3-1). Quarterback Len Dawson, 37, continues to lead the Chiefs' offense.
League Leaders: *Passer:* Bob Griese (Miami); *Rusher:* Floyd Little (Denver); *Receiver:* Paul Warfield (Miami); *Scorer:* Garo Yepremian (Miami).

Hall of Fame Inductees
Jim Brown, Bill Hewitt, Bruiser Kinard, Vince Lombardi, Andy Robustelli, Y.A. Tittle, Norm Van Brocklin

COLLEGE BOWLS & PRO CHAMPIONSHIPS

College Bowl Games
ROSE BOWL:
    Stanford 13, Michigan 12
SUGAR BOWL:
    Oklahoma 40, Auburn 22
COTTON BOWL:
    Penn State 30, Texas 6
ORANGE BOWL:
    Nebraska 38, Alabama 6
Arizona State, playing in the first Fiesta Bowl, beats Florida State at Tempe, Arizona, 45 to 38.

NFC
Playoffs: Dallas 20, Minnesota 12; San Francisco 24, Washington (Wild Card) 20.
Championship Game: Dallas 14, San Francisco 3. The Cowboy defense holds the 49ers to 61 yds rushing and no TDs. Quarterback Roger Staubach scrambles for 55 yds and passes for 103 to lead Dallas.

AFC
Playoffs: Miami 27, Kansas City 24 (2 OTs); Baltimore (Wild Card) 20, Cleveland 3.
Championship Game: Miami 21, Baltimore 0. Miami safety Dick Anderson makes a key interception of a Johnny Unitas pass and runs 62 yds for a TD in the 3d quarter.

Super Bowl VI
Dallas 24, Miami 3. Quarterback Roger Staubach, plus a strong Cowboy running attack (252 yds), leads Dallas to its first NFL championship. Lance Alworth and Mike Ditka score TDs on short passes and Duane Thomas runs over from the 3-yd line for the Cowboys' 3d TD. Miami's ground game is held to 80 yds.

1972

COLLEGE REGULAR SEASON

After a 21-year ban, freshmen are again allowed to play varsity football. Freshman Archie Griffin of Ohio State immediately serves notice by rushing 239 yds against North Carolina in the 2d game of the season.

USC (12-0-0) wins its 3d national championship in 11 years. Halfback Anthony Davis scores 6 TDs in the Notre Dame game as he and Sam Cunningham roll up the yardage behind a big Trojan line.

Wide receiver Johnny Rodgers of Nebraska wins the Heisman Trophy, setting an NCAA career record by gaining 5,586 total yds.

Conference Champions
BIG TEN: Michigan & Ohio State
BIG EIGHT: Oklahoma
PACIFIC EIGHT: USC
SOUTHEASTERN: Alabama
ATLANTIC COAST: North Carolina
SOUTHERN: East Carolina
SOUTHWEST: Texas (5th in a row)
IVY LEAGUE: Dartmouth

1972 All-American Team
(O = Offense; D = Defense)
E: Johnny Rodgers (O-Nebraska), Charles Young (O-UCLA), Bruce Bannon (D-Penn State), Willie Harper (D-Nebraska)
T: Jerry Sizemore (O-Texas), Pete Adams (O-USC), Dave Butz (D-Penn State), Greg Marx (D-Notre Dame)
G: Ron Rusnak (O-North Carolina), John Hannah (O-Alabama), Rich Glover (D-Oklahoma)
C: Tom Brahaney (O-Oklahoma)
LB: Randy Gradishar (D-Ohio State), Jamie Rotella (D-Tennessee)
B: Bert Jones (O-Louisiana State), Otis Armstrong (O-Purdue), Greg Pruitt (O-Oklahoma), Woodrow Green (O-Arizona State), Cullen Bryant (D-Colorado), Randy Logan (D-Michigan), Conrad Graham (D-Tennessee), Brad Van Pelt (D-Michigan State)

PROFESSIONAL REGULAR SEASON

NFC
Eastern Division Winner: Washington (11-3-0). The Redskins' "Over the Hill Gang" replaces Dallas as the Redskin defense holds rival teams to 218 points, best in the NFL.
Central Division Winner: Green Bay (10-4-0). John Brockington and MacArthur Lane rush for 1,898 yds to lead the Packers.
Western Division Winner: San Francisco (8-5-1). Quarterback Steve Spurrier fills in for injured John Brodie and hurls 18 TD passes in 7 games.
League Leaders: *Passer:* Fran Tarkenton (Minnesota); *Rusher:* Larry Brown (Washintgon); *Receiver:* Harold Jackson (Philadelphia); *Scorer:* Chester Marcol (Green Bay).

AFC
Eastern Division Winner: Miami (14-0-0). The Dolphins are the first undefeated, untied team in NFL history. Its "No-Name Defense" allows the fewest points in the NFL. Larry Csonka and Mercury Morris are the first teammates to gain 1,000 yds each in rushing for one season.
Central Division Winner: Pittsburgh (11-3-0). Quarterback Terry Bradshaw and fullback Franco Harris are offensive stars.
Western Division Winner: Oakland (10-3-1). Quarterback Daryle Lamonica has another good year and Marv Hubbard averages 5 yds per carry to lead the Raiders.
League Leaders: *Passer:* Daryle Lamonica (Oakland); *Rusher:* O.J. Simpson (Buffalo); *Receiver:* Rich Caster (New York); *Scorer:* Bobby Howfield (New York).

Hall of Fame Inductees
Lamar Hunt, Gino Marchetti, Ollie Matson, Ace Parker

COLLEGE BOWLS & PRO CHAMPIONSHIPS

College Bowl Games
ROSE BOWL:
 USC 42, Ohio State 17
SUGAR BOWL:
 Oklahoma 14, Penn State 0
COTTON BOWL:
 Texas 17, Alabama 13
ORANGE BOWL:
 Nebraska 40, Notre Dame 6

NFC
Playoffs: Dallas (Wild Card) 30, San Francisco 28; Washington 16, Green Bay 3.
Championship Game: Washington 26, Dallas 3. Curt Knight (4 field goals), reserve quarterback Bill Kilmer and halfback Larry Brown all star on offense for the Redskins. Washington's defense holds the Cowboys to 194 yds total offense.

AFC
Playoffs: Pittsburgh 13, Oakland 7; Miami 20, Cleveland (Wild Card) 14.
Championship Game: Miami 21, Pittsburgh 17. The Dolphins run their unbeaten, untied streak to 16 with a strong running attack (193 yds). The Steelers lose their star quarterback Terry Bradshaw for most of the game because of injury.

Super Bowl VII
Miami 14, Washington 7. Coach Don Shula leads the Dolphins to an unprecedented 17-0-0 season. Miami scores first on a pass from Bob Griese to Howard Twilley, then another on Jim Kiick's 1-yd plunge. The Redskins score in the 2d half only on Mike Bass's 49-yd return of Garo Yepremian's fumbled field goal try.

COLLEGE REGULAR SEASON

Notre Dame's first undefeated team since 1948 is named #1 in the nation after beating Alabama in the Sugar Bowl.

John Cappelletti becomes the first Penn State player to win the Heisman Trophy, finishing ahead of John Hicks (Ohio State).

In a game against New Mexico, Jay Miller of Brigham Young catches 22 passes (including 3 TDs) for a new major college record.

Conference Champions
BIG TEN: Ohio State & Michigan
BIG EIGHT: Oklahoma & Nebraska
SOUTHWEST: Texas
PACIFIC EIGHT: USC
WESTERN ATHLETIC: Arizona State
SOUTHEASTERN: Alabama
ATLANTIC COAST: N. C. State
SOUTHERN: East Carolina
IVY LEAGUE: Dartmouth

1973 All-American Team
Consensus All-American teams 1973 through 1988 courtesy of National Collegiate Athletic Association.
(O = Offense; D = Defense)
WR: Lynn Swann (USC)
TE: Dave Casper (Notre Dame)
L: John Hicks (O-Ohio State), Booker Brown (O-USC), Buddy Brown (O-Alabama); Bill Yoest (O-North Carolina State), John Dutton (D-Nebraska), Dave Gallagher (D-Michigan), Lucious Selmon (D- Oklahoma), Tony Cristiani (D-Miami, Fla.)
C: Bill Wyman (Texas)
LB: Randy Gradishar (Ohio State), Rod Shoate (Oklahoma), Richard Wood (USC)
B: Mike Townsend (D-Notre Dame), Artimus Parker (D-USC), Dave Brown (D-Michigan), Randy Rhino (D-Georgia Tech), Dave Jaynes (QB-Kansas), John Cappelletti (RB-Penn State), Roosevelt Leaks (RB-Texas), Woody Green (RB-Arizona State), Kermit Johnson (RB-UCLA)

PROFESSIONAL REGULAR SEASON

NFC
Eastern Division Winner: Dallas (10-4-0). Quarterback Roger Staubach stays healthy and Calvin Hill rushes for 1,142 yds.
Central Division Winner: Minnesota (12-2-0). A strong front four on defense and quarterback Fran Tarkenton on offense lead the Vikings to the playoffs.
Western Division Winner: Los Angeles (12-2-0). New coach Chuck Knox develops a strong ground game (2,925 yds) and leads the Rams into the playoffs.
League Leaders: *Passer:* Roman Gabriel (Philadelphia); *Rusher:* John Brockington (Green Bay); *Receiver:* Harold Carmichael (Philadelphia); *Scorer:* David Ray (Los Angeles).

AFC
Eastern Division Winner: Miami (12-2-0). Although their unbeaten string is broken at 19 games, the Dolphins are still the class of the AFC.
Central Division Winner: Cincinnati (10-4-0). Quarterback Ken Anderson has an All-Pro year as the Bengals win the last 6 games on their schedule.
Western Division Winner: Oakland (9-4-1). Quarterback Ken Stabler replaces Daryle Lamonica and leads the Raiders to the playoff.
League Leaders: *Passer:* Ken Anderson (Cincinnati); *Rusher:* O.J. Simpson (Buffalo). Simpson breaks Jim Brown's all-time season rushing record with 2,003 yds; *Receiver:* Isaac Curtis (Cincinnati); *Scorer:* Roy Gerela (Pittsburgh).

Hall of Fame Inductees
Raymond Berry, Jim Parker, Joe Schmidt

COLLEGE BOWLS & PRO CHAMPIONSHIPS

College Bowl Games
ROSE BOWL:
 Ohio State 42, USC 21
Behind 21-14 in the 3d quarter, Ohio State scores 28 unanswered points to win. Running backs Archie Griffin and Pete Johnson (3 TDs) pace the comeback.
SUGAR BOWL:
 Notre Dame 24, Alabama 23
COTTON BOWL:
 Nebraska 19, Texas 3
ORANGE BOWL:
 Penn State 16, Louisiana State 9

NFC
Playoffs: Minnesota 27, Washington (Wild Card) 20; Dallas 27, Los Angeles 16.
Championship Game: Minnesota 27, Dallas 10. Quarterback Fran Tarkenton outduels the Cowboys' Roger Staubach, who suffers 4 interceptions. The Viking ground game eats up yardage and time. Dallas runners gain only 50 yds.

AFC
Playoffs: Oakland 33, Pittsburgh (Wild Card) 14; Miami 34, Cincinnati 16.
Championship Game: Miami 27, Oakland 10. Larry Csonka races for 2 TDs and 117 yds to lead the Dolphins, who gain a total of 286 yds on the ground. Miami quarterback Bob Griese throws only 6 passes in the game.

Super Bowl VIII
Miami 24, Minnesota 7. Larry Csonka, with 145 yds rushing, carries the Dolphins to a second straight Super Bowl triumph. Ball control and a solid defense make the difference as the Vikings fall behind 17-0 at the half and cannot recover.

1974

COLLEGE REGULAR SEASON

USC, behind 24-0 with 2 minutes left in the 3d quarter, scores 55 consecutive points to beat Notre Dame, 55-24. USC's subsequent Rose Bowl victory over Ohio State, 18-7, earns it the nation's top ranking. Undefeated Oklahoma is under NCAA probation and is therefore not included in most polls. Archie Griffin, a junior at Ohio State, is the 5th underclassman to win the Heisman Trophy.

Vermont becomes the first state university to drop intercollegiate football, citing economic reasons.

Conference Champions
BIG TEN: Ohio State
PACIFIC EIGHT: USC
BIG EIGHT: Oklahoma
SOUTHEASTERN: Alabama
SOUTHWEST: Texas
SOUTHERN: Louisiana State
IVY LEAGUE: Yale

1974 All-American Team
(O = Offense; D = Defense)
WR: Pete Demmerle (Notre Dame)
TE: Bennie Cunningham (Clemson)
L: Kurt Shumacher (OT-Ohio State), Marvin Crenshaw (OT-Nebraska), Ken Huff (OG-North Carolina), John Roush (OG-Oklahoma), Gerry DiNardo (OG-Notre Dame), Randy White (D-Maryland), Mike Hartenstine (D-Penn State), Pat Donovan (D-Stanford), Jimmy Webb (D- Mississippi State), Leroy Cook (D-Alabama), Louie Kelcher (D-Southern Methodist), Rubin Carter (D-Miami, Fla.)
LB: Richard Wood (USC), Ken Bernich (Auburn), Woodrow Lowe (Alabama)
C: Steve Myers (Ohio State)
B: Dave Brown (D-Michigan), Pat Thomas (D-Texas A&M), John Provost (D-Holy Cross), Steve Bartkowski (QB-California), Archie Griffin (RB-Ohio State), Joe Washington (RB-Oklahoma), Anthony Davis (RB-USC)

PROFESSIONAL REGULAR SEASON

NFL
Eastern Conference Winner: St. Louis (10-4-0). Quarterback Jim Hart hurls 20 TD passes and runners Terry Metcalf and Jim Otis rush for 1,382 yds.
Central Division Winner: Minnesota (10-4-0). The Vikings are back in the playoffs behind quarterback Fran Tarkenton (2,592 yds passing) and a strong defense.
Western Division Winner: Los Angeles (10-4-0). The preseason favorites win easily in a weak division. Quarterback James Harris and halfback Larry McCutcheon (1,100 yds rushing) lead the offense.
League Leaders: *Passer:* Fran Tarkenton (Minnesota); *Rusher:* Larry McCutcheon (Los Angeles); *Receiver:* Drew Pearson (Dallas); *Scorer:* Chester Marcol (Green Bay).

AFC
Eastern Division Winner: Miami (11-3-0). Don Shula's Dolphins win their fourth division title in a row, but injuries to key players prevent another unbeaten season.
Central Division Winner: Pittsburgh (10-3-1). Steelers win on solid defense (189 points allowed, best in AFC) and ground attack (2,417 yds).
Western Division Winner: Oakland (12-2-0). Coach John Madden again produces a winner. Quarterback Ken Stabler passes for 2,400 yds and receiver Cliff Branch scores 13 TDs.
League Leaders: *Passer:* Ken Anderson (Cincinnati); *Rusher:* Otis Armstrong (Denver); *Receiver:* Cliff Branch (Oakland); *Scorer:* Roy Gerela (Pittsburgh).

Hall of Fame Inductees
Tony Canadeo, Bill George, Lou Groza, "Night Train" Lane

COLLEGE BOWLS & PRO CHAMPIONSHIPS

College Bowl Games:
ROSE BOWL:
   USC 18, Ohio State 17
SUGAR BOWL:
   Nebraska 13, Florida 10
COTTON BOWL:
   Penn State 41, Baylor 20
ORANGE BOWL:
   Notre Dame 13, Alabama 11

NFC
Playoffs: Minnesota 30, St. Louis 14; Los Angeles 19, Washington (Wild Card) 10.
Championship Game: Minnesota 14, Los Angeles 10. Quarterback James Harris outpasses Vikings' Fran Tarkenton, but fumbles, interceptions and penalties hurt the Rams, who are stopped 6 inches from the goal line in the 3d quarter.

AFC
Playoffs: Oakland 28, Miami 26; Pittsburgh 32, Buffalo (Wild Card) 14.
Championship Game: Pittsburgh 24, Oakland 13. The running of Franco Harris and Rocky Bleier (209 yds total) and a strong defense (Raiders are limited to 29 yds rushing) are too much for Oakland.

Super Bowl IX
Pittsburgh 16, Minnesota 6. The Vikings lose their 3d Super Bowl game, while the Steelers win on their first attempt. Franco Harris rushes for a Super Bowl record (158 yds). The only score in the 1st half is a safety by Pittsburgh. The Vikings score their only TD on a blocked punt recovery in the end zone.

COLLEGE REGULAR SEASON

Ohio State and Arizona State are the only major undefeated teams in the nation during the regular season. Other top-ranked teams are Oklahoma (which has its 37-game unbeaten streak broken by unranked Kansas), Alabama and UCLA.

Archie Griffin of Ohio State, after running a record 100 yds or more in 31 consecutive regular season games, becomes the first player to receive the Heisman Trophy twice. Chuck Muncie (California) and Ricky Bell (USC) finish second and third in the balloting.

Nolan Cromwell of Kansas, a defensive safety, starts at quarterback against Oregon State and breaks an NCAA record (for quarterbacks) by rushing for 294 yds in 28 carries.

Conference Champions
BIG TEN: Ohio State
BIG EIGHT: Oklahoma & Nebraska
PACIFIC EIGHT: UCLA
SOUTHEASTERN: Alabama
SOUTHWEST: Texas A&M
IVY LEAGUE: Harvard

1975 All-American Team
(O = Offense; D = Defense)
E: Steve Rivers (O-California), Larry Sievers (O- Tennessee), Leroy Cook (D-Alabama), Jimbo Elrod (D-Oklahoma)
L: Bob Simmons (O-Texas), Dennis Lick (O-Wisconsin), Randy Johnson (O-Georgia), Ted Smith (O-Ohio State), Lee Roy Selmon (D- Oklahoma), Steve Niehaus (D-Notre Dame), Dewey Selmon (D-Oklahoma)
C: Rik Bonness (Nebraska)
LB: Ed Simonini (Texas A&M), Greg Buttle (Penn State), Sammy Green (Florida)
B: Chet Moeller (D-Navy), Tim Fox (D-Ohio State), Pat Thomas (D-Texas A&M), John Sciarra (QB-UCLA), Archie Griffin (RB-Ohio State), Ricky Bell (RB-USC), Chuck Muncie (RB-California)

PROFESSIONAL REGULAR SEASON

NFC
Eastern Division Winner: St. Louis (11-3-0). Jim Otis and Terry Metcalf rush for 1,892 yds and Mel Gray grabs 48 passes for 11 TDs to lead the Cardinal offense.
Central Division Winner: Minnesota (12-2-0). The Vikings win for the 3d year in a row. Quarterback Fran Tarkenton tosses 25 TD passes and gains 2,994 yds in the air.
Western Division Winner: Los Angeles (12-2-0). The Rams win easily with a strong ground game and the best defense in the NFC (only 135 points allowed in 14 games).
League Leaders: *Passer:* Fran Tarkenton (Minnesota); *Rusher:* Chuck Foreman (Minnesota); *Receiver:* Mel Gray (St. Louis); *Scorer:* Chuck Foreman (Minnesota).

AFC
Eastern Division Winner: Baltimore (10-4-0). After losing 4 out of 5 games, the Colts win 9 straight to take the division title from Miami. Quarterback Bert Jones (2,483 yds passing) and halfback Lydell Mitchell (1,193 yds rushing) carry the offense.
Central Division Winner: Pittsburgh (12-2-0). Steeler defense yields the fewest points (162) in the AFC. Quarterback Terry Bradshaw passes for 2,055 yds and Franco Harris rushes for 1,246 yds.
Western Division Winner: Oakland (11-3-0). The Raiders win easily in a weak division. George Blanda, 47, retires after a 27- year career with 2,002 points scored, most ever in pro football.
League Leaders: *Passer:* Ken Anderson (Cincinnati); *Rusher:* O.J. Simpson (Buffalo); *Receiver:* Ken Burrough (Houston); *Scorer:* O.J. Simpson (Buffalo).

Hall of Fame Inductees
Rosey Brown, George Conner, Dante Lavelli, Lenny Moore

COLLEGE BOWLS & PRO CHAMPIONSHIPS

College Bowl Games
ROSE BOWL:
  UCLA 23, Ohio State 10
SUGAR BOWL:
  Alabama 13, Penn State 6
COTTON BOWL:
  Arkansas 31, Georgia 10
ORANGE BOWL:
  Oklahoma 14, Michigan 6

NFC
Playoffs: Los Angeles 35, St. Louis 23; Dallas (Wild Card) 17, Minnesota 14.
Championship Game: Dallas 37, Los Angeles 7. Dallas builds a 21-0 lead at the half and coasts to victory. Quarterback Roger Staubach passes for 220 yds and tosses 3 TD passes. The Cowboy defense limits the Rams to 22 yds rushing and makes 3 interceptions.

AFC
Pittsburgh 28, Baltimore 10; Oakland 31, Cincinnati (Wild Card) 28.
Championship Game: Pittsburgh 16, Oakland 10. All but 3 points in the game are scored in the 4th quarter as the Raiders lose their 6th championship game in the last 8 years. Quarterback Terry Bradshaw completes 15 of 25 passes for 215 yds, including a 20-yd toss to John Stallworth.

Super Bowl X
Pittsburgh 21, Dallas 17. The Steelers come from behind with 14 points in the 4th quarter to win their 2d straight Super Bowl. Lynn Swann catches 4 Terry Bradshaw passes for 161 yds and Roy Gerela boots 2 field goals. Roger Staubach heaves 2 TD passes for the Cowboys in a losing cause.

COLLEGE REGULAR SEASON

Under coach Johnny Majors, Pittsburgh goes through its season undefeated. Halfback Tony Dorsett sets 11 NCAA records and becomes the first runner to gain more than 6,000 yds in his college career. Dorsett also wins the Heisman Trophy, easily beating out Ricky Bell (USC) and Rob Lytle (Michigan).

Rutgers and Maryland also enjoy undefeated seasons but are unranked because of their weaker schedules.

Tony Franklin of Texas A&M kicks 2 record-breaking field goals in the same game (64 yds and 65 yds) to set an NCAA record.

Conference Champions
BIG TEN: Michigan
BIG EIGHT: Colorado, Oklahoma & Oklahoma A&M (tied)
PACIFIC EIGHT: USC
SOUTHWEST: Houston
ATLANTIC COAST: Maryland
SOUTHEASTERN: Georgia
IVY LEAGUE: Yale & Brown

1976 All-American Team
(O = Offense; D = Defense)
E: Ken MacAfee (O-Notre Dame), Larry Sievers (O-Tennessee), Ross Browner (D-Notre Dame), Bob Brudzinski (D-Ohio State)
T: Mike Vaughan (O-Oklahoma), Chris Ward (O-Ohio State), Wilson Whitley (D-Houston), Gary Jeter (D-USC), Joe Campbell (D- Maryland)
G: Joel Parrish (O-Georgia), Mark Donahue (O-Michigan), Al Romano (D-Pittsburgh)
C: Derrel Gofourth (Oklahoma)
LB: Robert Jackson (Texas A&M), Jerry Robinson (UCLA)
B: Bill Armstrong (D-Wake Forest), Gary Green (D-Baylor), Dennis Thurman (D-USC), Dave Butterfield (D-Nebraksa), Tommy Kramer (QB-Rice), Tony Dorsett (RB-Pittsburgh), Ricky Bell (RB-USC), Rob Lytle (RB-Michigan)
K: Tony Franklin (Texas A&M)

PROFESSIONAL REGULAR SEASON

NFC
Eastern Division Winner: Dallas (11-3-0). Lack of a consistent ground game is the Cowboys' only weakness. Roger Staubach completes 58% of passes attempted for 2,715 yds.
Central Division Winner: Minnesota (11-2-1). Vikings win their 4th division title in a row. Quarterback Fran Tarkenton passes 412 times for 2,966 yds and Chuck Foreman rushes for 1,155 more.
Western Division Winner: Los Angeles (10-3-1). The Rams take their 4th straight NFC West title. Larry McCutcheon and John Cappelletti rush for 1,876 yds.
League Leaders: *Passer:* Fran Tarkenton (Minnesota); *Rusher:* Walter Payton (Chicago); *Receiver:* Sammy White (Minnesota); *Scorer:* Mark Moseley (Washington).

AFC
Eastern Division Winner: Baltimore (11-3-0). Colts repeat as AFC East champs. Quarterback Bert Jones passes for 3,104 yds and 24 TDs. Lydell Mitchell rushes for 1,200 yds. Baltimore's defense is #1 in the league against rushing.
Central Division Winner: Pittsburgh (10-4-0). Steeler backs Franco Harris and Rocky Bleier rush for 2,164 yds to lead the Steelers' potent offense (24.4 points per game).
Western Division Winner: Oakland (13-1-0). The Raiders capture their 5th title in a row, losing only to New England. Quarterback Ken Stabler is ranked #1 in the AFC.
League Leaders: *Passer:* Ken Stabler (Oakland); *Rusher:* O.J. Simpson (Buffalo). Simpson breaks his own NFL record with 273 yds rushing in one game (Nov. 25.); *Receiver:* Roger Carr (Baltimore); *Scorer:* Toni Linhart (Baltimore).

Hall of Fame Inductees
Ray Flaherty, Len Ford, Jim Taylor

COLLEGE BOWLS & PRO CHAMPIONSHIPS

College Bowl Games
ROSE BOWL:
USC 14, Michigan 6
SUGAR BOWL:
Pittsburgh 27, Georgia 3
COTTON BOWL:
Houston 30, Maryland 21
ORANGE BOWL:
Ohio State 27, Colorado 10

NFC
Playoffs: Minnesota 35, Washington (Wild Card) 20; Los Angeles 14, Dallas 12.
Championship Game: Minnesota 24, Los Angeles 13. Bobby Bryant, Viking defensive back, picks up a blocked field goal attempt by the Rams in the 1st quarter and races 90 yds for a TD. Minnesota goes on to clinch its 3d NFC championship in 4 years.

AFC
Playoffs: Oakland 24, New England (Wild Card) 20; Pittsburgh 40, Baltimore 14.
Championship Game: Oakland 24, Pittsburgh 7. With star running backs Franco Harris and Rocky Bleier out with injuries, the Steelers are no match for the Raider defense. Ken Stabler throws 2 TD passes to clinch the first AFC championship in Oakland in 7 tries.

Super Bowl XI
Oakland 32, Minnesota 14. The Vikings lose their 4th Super Bowl as the Raiders erupt for 16 points in the 2d quarter. Clarence Davis rushes for 137 yds and Willie Brown returns an intercepted pass 75 yds for a TD to lead the Raiders to their first Super Bowl win.

COLLEGE REGULAR SEASON

Texas is the only major undefeated college team during the regular season—but loses its #1 ranking to Notre Dame at the Cotton Bowl. Earl Campbell leads the Longhorns with 19 TDs and 1,744 yds rushing on 267 carries (6.1-yd average). He also wins the Heisman Trophy over Terry Miller of Oklahoma State.

Other top-ranked teams include Alabama, Penn State, Ohio State, Arkansas, Kentucky, Texas A&M and Stanford.

Steve Little (Arkansas) and Russell Erxleben (Texas) both kick record-breaking 67-yd field goals.

Conference Champions
BIG TEN: Michigan
BIG EIGHT: Oklahoma
PACIFIC EIGHT: Washington
SOUTHWEST: Texas
SOUTHEASTERN: Alabama
IVY LEAGUE: Yale

1977 All-American Team
(O = Offense; D = Defense)
WR: John Jefferson (Arizona State), Ozzie Newsome (Alabama)
TE: Ken McAfee (Notre Dame)
L: Ross Browner (D-Notre Dame), Art Still (D-Kentucky), Brad Shearer (D-Texas), Randy Holloway (D-Pittsburgh), Dee Hardison (D-North Carolina), Chris Ward (O-Ohio State), Dan Irons (O-Texas Tech), Mark Donahue (O-Michigan), Leotis Harris (O-Arkansas)
C: Tom Brzoza (Pittsburgh)
LB: Jerry Robinson (UCLA), Tom Cousineau (Ohio State), Gary Spani (Kansas State)
B: Dennis Thurman (D-USC), Zac Henderson (D-Oklahoma), Luther Bradley (D-Notre Dame), Bob Jury (D-Pittsburgh), Guy Benjamin (QB-Stanford), Earl Campbell (RB-Texas), Terry Miller (RB-Oklahoma State), Charles Alexander (RB-Louisiana State)
K: Steve Little (RB-Arkansas)

PROFESSIONAL REGULAR SEASON

NFC
Eastern Division Winner: Dallas (12-2-0). The Cowboys win their 5th division title in the last 8 years. Quarterback Roger Staubach is ranked #1 in NFC and rookie running back Tony Dorsett rushes 1,007 yds.
Central Division Winner: Minnesota (9-5-0). The Vikings take their 5th division title in a row despite losing star quarterback Fran Tarkenton (broken leg) for the last 5 games.
Western Division Winner: Los Angeles (10-4-0). The Rams win their 5th straight NFC West title behind quarterback Pat Haden.
League Leaders: *Passer:* Roger Staubach (Dallas); *Rusher:* Walter Payton (Chicago); *Receiver:* Mel Gray (St. Louis); *Scorer:* Walter Payton (Chicago).

AFC
Eastern Division Winner: Baltimore (10-4-0). The Colts win their 3d division title in a row. Lydell Mitchell rushes for 1,159 yds and snags 71 passes.
Central Division Winner: Pittsburgh (9-5-0). The Steelers are division champs for the 4th year in a row. Quarterback Terry Bradshaw's passes to Lynn Swann and John Stallworth are key factors.
Western Division Winner: Denver (12-2-0). The Broncos win their first division title behind veteran quarterback Craig Morton.
League Leaders: *Passer:* Bob Griese (Miami); *Rusher:* Mark van Eeghen (Oakland); *Receiver:* Lydell Mitchell (Baltimore); *Scorer:* Errol Mann (Oakland).

Hall of Fame Inductees
Frank Gifford, Forrest Gregg, Gale Sayers, Bart Starr, Bill Willis

COLLEGE BOWLS & PRO CHAMPIONSHIPS

College Bowl Games
ROSE BOWL:
  Washington 27, Michigan 20
SUGAR BOWL:
  Alabama 35, Ohio State 6
COTTON BOWL:
  Notre Dame 38, Texas 10
ORANGE BOWL:
  Arkansas 31, Oklahoma 6

NFC
Playoffs: Dallas 37, Chicago (Wild Card) 7; Minnesota 14, Los Angeles 7.
Championship Game: Dallas 23, Minnesota 6. Without ailing quarterback Fran Tarkenton, the Viking offense is unable to score a TD as the Cowboys move ahead, 16-6, at halftime and are never threatened. Dallas defense recovers 3 Viking fumbles, intercepts a Bob Lee pass, and holds Chuck Foreman to 59 yds rushing.

AFC
Playoffs: Oakland (Wild Card) 37, Baltimore 31 (2 OTs). Raider quarterback Stabler passes for 345 yds, a record.
Championship Game: Denver 20, Oakland 17. The Broncos upset the Super Bowl champions despite the Raiders' 14-point spurt in the 4th quarter. Denver receiver Haven Moses snares 5 Craig Morton passes for 168 yds and 2 TDs.

Super Bowl XII
Dallas 27, Denver 10. The Cowboys move in front, 13-0, at halftime and are never threatened. Butch Johnson's TD on a 46-yd pass from quarterback Roger Staubach in the 3d quarter clinches the 2d Super Bowl victory for Dallas.

1978

COLLEGE REGULAR SEASON

Eddie Lee Ivery of Georgia Tech gains a record 356 yds in 23 carries against the Air Force Academy (Nov. 11). The following week, Frank Mordica of Vanderbilt rushes 321 yds against the same Air Force team for a total of 677 yds in consecutive games.

Oklahoma running back Billy Sims wins the Heisman Trophy. Chuck Fusina (Penn State) and Rick Leach (Michigan) finish second and third in the balloting.

Alabama and USC tie for first in the football polls after Alabama defeats previously unbeaten Penn State in the Sugar Bowl.

Conference Champions
BIG TEN: Michigan
BIG EIGHT: Oklahoma & Nebraska
ATLANTIC COAST: Clemson
PACIFIC EIGHT: USC
SOUTHWEST: Houston
SOUTHEASTERN: Alabama

1978 All-American Team
(O = Offense; D = Defense)
WR: Emanuel Tolbert (Southern Methodist)
TE: Kellen Winslow (Missouri)
L: Keith Dorney (O-Penn State), Kelvin Clark (O-Nebraska), Pat Howell (O-USC), Greg Roberts (O-Oklahoma), Al Harris (D-Arizona State), Bruce Clark (D-Penn State), Hugh Green (D-Pittsburgh), Mike Bell (D-Colorado State), Marty Lyons (D-Alabama)
C: Dave Huffman (Notre Dame)
LB: Bob Golic (Notre Dame), Jerry Robinson (UCLA), Tom Cousineau (Ohio State)
B: Johnnie Johnson (D-Texas), Kenny Easley (D-UCLA), Jeff Nixon (D-Richmond), Chuck Fusina (QB-Penn State), Billy Sims (RB-Oklahoma), Charles White (RB-USC), Ted Brown (RB-North Carolina State), Charles Alexander (RB-Louisiana State)

PROFESSIONAL REGULAR SEASON

The NFL season is expanded from 14 to 16 games. A second "Wild Card" berth is added to the playoff system.

NFC
Eastern Division Winner: Dallas (12-4-0). Quarterback Roger Staubach has an All-Pro year (25 TD passes and 3,190 yds passing).
Central Division Winner: Minnesota (8-7-1). Quarterback Fran Tarkenton, 38, ends his 18-year career with 25 TD passes and 3,408 yds.
Western Division Winner: Los Angeles (12-4-0). The Rams capture their 6th division title in a row.
League Leaders: *Passer:* Roger Staubach (Dallas); *Rusher:* Walter Payton (Chicago); *Receiver:* Harold Carmichael (Philadelphia); *Scorer:* Frank Corral (Los Angeles).

AFC
Eastern Division Winner: New England (11-5-0). The Patriots finally make the playoffs behind a good running attack (3,165 yds). All-Pro defensive back Mike Haynes leads the defense.
Central Division Winner: Pittsburgh (14-2-0). The Steelers easily win their 5th straight division title behind Terry Bradshaw's passing (28 TD passes) and the "Steel Curtain" defense (best in the NFL).
Western Division Winner: Denver (10-6-0). The Broncos repeat as division champs. The "Orange Crush" defense allows less than 13 points per game. Rick Upchurch returns 36 punts for 493 yds.
League Leaders: *Passer:* Terry Bradshaw (Pittsburgh); *Rusher:* Earl Campbell (Houston); *Receiver:* Wes Walker (New York); *Scorer:* Pat Leahy (New York).

Hall of Fame Inductees
Lance Alworth, Weeb Ewbank, Tuffy Leemans, Ray Nitschke, Larry Wilson

COLLEGE BOWLS & PRO CHAMPIONSHIPS

College Bowl Games
ROSE BOWL:
  USC 17, Michigan 10
SUGAR BOWL:
  Alabama 14, Penn State 7
COTTON BOWL:
  Notre Dame 35, Houston 34
ORANGE BOWL:
  Oklahoma 31, Nebraska 24
In the first Holiday Bowl, Navy defeats Brigham Young, 23-16. At the Gator Bowl, Ohio State coach Woody Hayes punches Clemson defender Charlie Bauman after he intercepts an Ohio State pass to ruin Ohio State's chances. Hayes is later fired. His 33-year career ends with 238 wins, 72 losses, 10 ties, plus 2 national championships.

NFC
Playoffs: Atlanta 14, Philadelphia 13 (Wild Card); Los Angeles 34, Minnesota 10; Dallas 27, Atlanta 20.
Championship Game: Dallas 28, Los Angeles 0. After a scoreless first half, the Cowboys explode for 21 points in the 4th quarter. Quarterback Roger Staubach throws 2 TD passes and Tom Henderson returns an interception 68 yds for a TD.

AFC
Playoffs: Houston 17, Miami 9 (Wild Card); Pittsburgh 33, Denver 10; Houston 31, New England 14.
Championship Game: Pittsburgh 34, Houston 5. Steeler quarterback Terry Bradshaw heaves 2 TD passes and Pittsburgh's "Steel Curtain" defense holds Houston star Earl Campbell to 62 yds rushing.

Super Bowl XIII
Pittsburgh 35, Dallas 31. In the first rematch in Super Bowl history, Pittsburgh quarterback Terry Bradshaw tosses 4 TD passes (a Super Bowl record). Dallas quarterback Roger Staubach (3 TD passes) also excels in a close, exciting game. The Steelers are the first team to win 3 Super Bowls.

COLLEGE REGULAR SEASON

Alabama is #1 in the nation, with USC a close second. Ohio State, Florida State, Arkansas, Houston, Oklahoma and Pittsburgh are other top-ranked teams.

Billy Simms of Oklahoma (22 TDs) and Charles White of USC (180-yd rushing average per game) battle it out for the Heisman Trophy. White is the winner. Marc Wilson of Brigham Young (29 TDs, 250 completions) comes in third.

Utah State and San Jose State play the highest-scoring tie game (48-48) in major college football history.

Conference Champions
BIG TEN: Ohio State
BIG EIGHT: Oklahoma
PACIFIC COAST: San Jose State
PACIFIC TEN: USC
SOUTHWEST: Arkansas & Houston
ATLANTIC COAST: N. C. State
IVY LEAGUE: Yale

1979 All-American Team
(O = Offense; D = Defense)
WR: Ken Margerum (Stanford)
TE: Junior Miller (Nebraska)
L: Greg Kolenda (O-Arkansas), Jim Bunch (O-Alabama), Brad Budde (O-USC), Ken Fritz (O-Ohio State), Hugh Green (D-Pittsburgh), Steve McMichael (D-Texas), Bruce Clark (D-Penn State), Jim Stuckey (D-Clemson), Ron Simmons (D-Florida State)
C: Jim Ritcher (North Carolina State)
LB: George Cumby (Oklahoma), Ron Simpkins (Michigan), Mike Singletary (Baylor)
B: Kenny Easley (D-UCLA), Johnnie Johnson (D-Texas), Roland James (D-Tennessee), Marc Wilson (QB-Brigham Young), Charles White (RB-USC), Billy Sims (RB-Oklahoma), Vagas Ferguson (RB-Notre Dame)
K: Jim Miller (P-Mississippi), Dale Castro (PK-Maryland)

PROFESSIONAL REGULAR SEASON

NFC
Eastern Division Winner: Dallas (11-5-0). The Cowboys capture their 4th division title in a row. Quarterback Roger Staubach announces his retirement at the end of his 11th season with Dallas. Halfback Tony Dorsett gains over 1,000 yds for the 3d straight year.
Central Division Winner: Tampa Bay (10-6-0). The Buccaneers make the playoffs for the first time. Ricky Bell runs for 1,263 yds; the defense holds the opposition to 1,873 yds.
Western Division Winner: Los Angeles (9-7-0). The Rams make the playoffs for the 7th straight year. Vince Ferragamo takes over at quarterback in mid-season and leads the Rams to the title.
League Leaders: *Passer:* Roger Staubach (Dallas); *Rusher:* Walter Payton (Chicago); *Receiver:* Ahmad Rashad (Minnesota); *Scorer:* Mark Moseley (Washington).

AFC
Eastern Division Winner: Miami (10-6-0). Injured quarterback Bob Griese comes off the bench to help Miami win 2 key games.
Central Division Winner: Pittsburgh (12-4-0). The Steelers capture their 6th straight division title. Quarterback Terry Bradshaw tosses 26 TD passes and gains 3,724 yds in the air.
Western Division Winner: San Diego (12-4-0). The Chargers quarterback Dan Fouts sets an NFL record for passing yardage in one season (4,082) and completes 24 TD passes.
League Leaders: *Passer:* Dan Fouts (San Diego); *Rusher:* Earl Campbell (Houston); *Receiver:* Steve Largent (Seattle); *Scorer:* John Smith (New England).

Hall of Fame Inductees
Dick Butkus, Yale Lary, Ron Mix, Johnny Unitas

COLLEGE BOWLS & PRO CHAMPIONSHIPS

College Bowl Games
ROSE BOWL:
USC 17, Ohio State 16
SUGAR BOWL:
Alabama 24, Arkansas 9
COTTON BOWL:
Houston 17, Nebraska 14
ORANGE BOWL:
Oklahoma 24, Florida State 7

NFC
Playoffs: Philadelphia 27, Chicago 17 (Wild Card); Tampa Bay 24, Philadelphia 17; Los Angeles 21, Dallas 19.
Championship Game: Los Angeles 9, Tampa Bay 0. Frank Corral's 3 field goals represent all the scoring as the Rams' defense stops the Bucs cold on the ground (92 yds) and in the air (5 completions out of 27).

AFC
Playoffs: Houston 13, Denver 7 (Wild Card); Houston 17, San Diego 14; Pittsburgh 34, Miami 14.
Championship Game: Pittsburgh 27, Houston 13. The Steelers win their 4th AFC championship in the past 6 years. Quarterback Terry Bradshaw tosses 2 TD passes and the defense holds Earl Campbell to 15 yds in 17 running plays.

Super Bowl XIV
Pittsburgh 31, Los Angeles 19. The Steelers win their 4th Super Bowl and 2d in a row. Trailing 19-17 after 3 quarters, Pittsburgh scores 2 TDs in the 4th quarter to win. John Stallworth grabs a Terry Bradshaw pass and races 73 yds to put the Steelers in front to stay.

Coach **Don Shula** consults with his defensive captain, Nick Buoniconti, during the Miami Dolphins perfect season of 1972.
Malcom W. Emmons

Roger Staubach, former All-American at Navy, goes to work for the Dallas Cowboys.
Malcom W. Emmons

Probably the most elusive quarterback in NFL history, **Fran Tarkenton** of the Minnesota Vikings gets set to uncork a long scoring pass. Malcom W. Emmons

The Chicago Bears' superstar, **Walter Payton,** scrambles for more yardage.
Malcom W. Emmons

Terry Bradshaw, Pittsburgh Steeler quarterback for 13 years, hands off to his running back. Malcom W. Emmons

O.J. Simpson, former Heisman Trophy winner at USC, heads for the goal line for the Buffalo Bills.
Malcom W. Emmons

71

COLLEGE REGULAR SEASON

Oklahoma thrashes Colorado, 82-42, in the highest-scoring game in major college history. The Sooners' total rushing yardage (758 in 73 attempts) is also a single-game record.

Georgia, led by freshman halfback Herschel Walker, is the only undefeated major college team.

Jim McMahon, Brigham Young quarterback, sets records for most passing yardage in a season (4,571) and most TD passes (47).

George Rogers of South Carolina (1,781 yds rushing) wins the Heisman Trophy, beating out Herschel Walker (Georgia).

Conference Champions
BIG TEN: Michigan
BIG EIGHT: Oklahoma
PACIFIC TEN: Washington
SOUTHEASTERN: Georgia
SOUTHWEST: Baylor
ATLANTIC COAST: North Carolina
WESTERN ATHLETIC: BYU
IVY LEAGUE: Yale

1980 All-American Team
(O = Offense; D = Defense)
WR: Ken Margerum (Stanford)
TE: Dave Young (Purdue)
L: Mark May (O-Pittsburgh), Keith Van Horne (O-USC), Nick Eyre (O-Brigham Young), Louis Oubre (O-Oklahoma), Randy Schleusener (O-Nebraska), Hugh Green (D-Pittsburgh), E.J. Junior (D-Alabama), Kenneth Sims (D-Texas), Leonard Mitchell (D-Houston), Ron Simmons (D-Florida State)
C: John Scully (Notre Dame)
LB: Mike Singletary (Baylor), Lawrence Taylor (North Carolina), David Little (Florida), Bob Crable (Notre Dame)
B: Kenny Easley (D-UCLA), Ronnie Lott (D-USC), John Simmons (Southern Methodist), Mark Herrmann (QB-Purdue), George Rogers (RB-South Carolina), Herschel Walker (RB-Georgia), Jarvis Redwine (RB-Nebraska)

PROFESSIONAL REGULAR SEASON

NFC
Eastern Division Winner: Philadelphia (12-4-0). The Eagles nose out Dallas for their first division title. Quarterback Ron Jaworski throws 257 completions for 3,529 yds and 27 TDs.
Central Division Winner: Minnesota (9-7-0). The Vikings barely beat out the Detroit Lions for the title, with new quarterback Tommy Kramer passing for 3,582 yds.
Western Division Winner: Atlanta (12-4-0). The Falcons win their first division title behind quarterback Steve Bartkowski (3,544 yds and 31 TDs) and the running of William Andrews (1,308 yds).
League Leaders: *Passer:* Ron Jaworski (Philadelphia); *Rusher:* Walter Payton (Chicago); *Receiver:* James Lofton (Green Bay); *Scorer:* Ed Murray (Detroit).

AFC
Eastern Division Winner: Buffalo (11-5-0). The Bills make the playoffs for the first time in 6 years. Rookie halfback Joe Cribbs rushes for 1,185 yds. Buffalo's pass defense is the best in the AFC.
Central Division Winner: Cleveland (11-5-0). The Browns edge the Oilers in a tie-breaker to win their first AFC title since '71. Quarterback Brian Sipe has the best AFC record: 4,132 yds and 30 TDs.
Western Division Winner: San Diego (11-5-0). Dan Fouts passes for 30 TDs and 4,716 yds, best in the AFC. Kellen Winslow, John Jefferson and Charlie Joiner are all 1,000-yd receivers.
League Leaders: *Passer:* Brian Sipe (Cleveland); *Rusher:* Earl Campbell (Houston); *Receiver:* John Jefferson (San Diego); *Scorer:* John Smith (New England).

Hall of Fame Inductees
Herb Adderley, Deacon Jones, Bob Lilly, Jim Otto

COLLEGE BOWLS & PRO CHAMPIONSHIPS

College Bowl Games
ROSE BOWL:
  Michigan 23, Washington 6
SUGAR BOWL:
  Georgia 17, Notre Dame 10
COTTON BOWL:
  Alabama 30, Baylor 2
ORANGE BOWL:
  Oklahoma 18, Florida State 17

NFC
Playoffs: Dallas 34, Los Angeles 13 (Wild Card); Philadelphia 31, Minnesota 16; Dallas 30, Atlanta 27.
Championship Game: Philadelphia 20, Dallas 7. After winning 2 playoff games as a "Wild Card" team, the Cowboys come up short in the championship. Tied 7-7 at the half, the Eagles hold Dallas scoreless from then on. Wilbert Montgomery rushes for 194 yds to lead the Eagle offense.

AFC
Playoffs: Oakland 27, Houston 7 (Wild Card); San Diego 20, Buffalo 14; Oakland 14, Cleveland 12.
Championship Game: Oakland 34, San Diego 27. "Wild Card" Oakland makes it to the Super Bowl behind quarterback Jim Plunkett (14 completions out of 18 attempts and 2 TDs). Dan Fouts completes 22 passes for 336 yds in a losing cause.

Super Bowl XV
Oakland 27, Philadelphia 10. "Wild Card" Raiders win their second Super Bowl. Quarterback Jim Plunkett throws 2 TD passes in the 1st quarter to lead Oakland. Eagle quarterback Ron Jaworski completes 18 passes for 291 yds, but 3 passes are picked off by Rod Martin, Raider linebacker, to stop Eagle drives.

COLLEGE REGULAR SEASON

Clemson (12-0) boasts the only undefeated team among all major colleges, thanks to a 22-15 win over Nebraska in the Orange Bowl. Other top-ranked teams include Michigan, Notre Dame, USC, Texas, Penn State and Pittsburgh.

Marcus Allen of USC is named winner of the Heisman Trophy, with Herschel Walker (Georgia) and Jim McMahon (Brigham Young) finishing 2d and 3d in the balloting.

Conference Champions

BIG TEN: Iowa & Ohio State
PACIFIC TEN: Washington
SOUTHEAST: Georgia & Alabama
BIG EIGHT: Nebraska
SOUTHWEST: Southern Methodist
ATLANTIC COAST: Clemson
MISSOURI VALLEY: Tulsa
WESTERN ATHLETIC: BYU
IVY LEAGUE: Yale & Dartmouth

1981 All-American Team

(O = Offense; D = Defense)
WR: Anthony Carter (Michigan)
TE: Tim Wrightman (UCLA)
L: Sean Farrell (O-Penn State), Roy Foster (O-USC), Terry Crouch (O-Oklahoma), Ed Muransky (O-Michigan), Terry Tausch (O-Texas), Kurt Becker (O-Michigan), Billy Ray Smith (D-Arkansas), Kenneth Sims (D-Texas), Andre Tippett (D-Iowa), Tim Krumrie (D-Wisconsin)
C: Dave Rimington (Nebraska)
LB: Bob Crable (Notre Dame), Jeff Davis (Clemson), Sal Sunseri (Pittsburgh)
B: Tommy Wilcox (D-Alabama), Mike Richardson (D-Arizona State), Terry Kinard (D-Clemson), Fred Marion (D-Miami, Fla.), Jim McMahon (QB-Brigham Young), Marcus Allen (RB-USC), Herschel Walker (RB-Georgia)
K: Reggie Roby (P-Iowa)

PROFESSIONAL REGULAR SEASON

NFC

Eastern Division Winner: Dallas (12-4-0). The Cowboys regain the division title behind new quarterback Danny White (3,098 yds and 22 TD passes). Tony Dorsett rushes for 1,646 yds.
Central Division Winner: Tampa Bay (9-7-0). The Buccaneers make the playoffs despite a mediocre offense and an average defense.
Western Division Winner: San Francisco (13-3-0). Quarterback Joe Montana has a 64% completion average and 3,565 yds passing.
League Leaders: *Passer:* Joe Montana (San Francisco); *Rusher:* George Rogers (New Orleans); *Receiver:* Al Jenkins (Atlanta); *Scorer:* Ed Murray (Detroit) and Rafael Septien (Dallas).

AFC

Eastern Division Winner: Miami (11-4-1). The Dolphin defense allows the fewest points in the AFC (275). Tony Nathan and Andra Franklin rush for combined 1,493 yds.
Central Division Winner: Cincinnati (12-4-0). Number-one-ranked quarterback Ken Anderson (63% pass completion average and 29 TD passes) spearheads the attack. Rookie Chris Collinsworth is his top receiver.
Western Division Winner: San Diego (10-6-0). The Chargers repeat as AFC West champs. Quarterback Dan Fouts' passing accounts for 4,802 yds passing and 33 TDs.
League Leaders: *Passer:* Ken Anderson (Cincinnati); *Rusher:* Earl Campbell (Houston); *Receiver:* Kellen Winslow (San Diego); *Scorer:* Nick Lowery (Kansas City) and Jim Breech (Cincinnati).

Hall of Fame Inductees

Red Badgro, George Blanda, Willie Davis, Jim Ringo

COLLEGE BOWLS & PRO CHAMPIONSHIPS

College Bowl Games

ROSE BOWL:
  Washington 28, Iowa 0
SUGAR BOWL:
  Pittsburgh 24, Georgia 20
COTTON BOWL:
  Texas 14, Alabama 12
ORANGE BOWL:
  Clemson 22, Nebraska 15

NFC

Playoffs: New York 27, Philadelphia 21 (Wild Card); Dallas 38, Tampa Bay 0; San Francisco 38, New York 24.
Championship Game: San Francisco 28, Dallas 27. 49er quarterback Joe Montana's passing attack (3 TD passes and 286 yds) and Dwight Clark's 4th quarter TD completion combine to nip Dallas.

AFC

Playoffs: Buffalo 31, New York 27 (Wild Card); San Diego 41, Miami 38 (OT); Cincinnati 28, Buffalo 21.
Championship Game: Cincinnati 27, San Diego 7. The Bengals win a trip to their first Super Bowl. The game is played despite a wind chill factor of -59° at Riverfront Stadium. Quarterback Ken Anderson tosses 2 TD passes and Jim Breech kicks 2 field goals to lead the Cincinnati offense.

Super Bowl XVI

San Francisco 26, Cincinnati 21. The 49ers build a 20-0 lead at halftime and hold off the Bengals in the 2d half to win their first Super Bowl. Bengal quarterback Ken Anderson passes for 300 yds and 2 TDs in a losing cause. Ray Wersching boots 4 field goals for the 49ers.

COLLEGE REGULAR SEASON

After defeating Georgia in the Sugar Bowl, Penn State (11-1- 0) is named the national champion for the first time in coach Joe Paterno's 17-year career there.

Herschel Walker, a junior at Georgia, takes the Heisman Trophy (the 7th under-classman so honored).

With 4 seconds left on the clock and trailing Stanford, 20-19, California takes the kickoff and, after a series of frantic laterals, runs it back 57 yds for a "miracle" TD.

Conference Champions
BIG TEN: Michigan
BIG EIGHT: Nebraska
SOUTHWEST: Southern Methodist
ATLANTIC COAST: Clemson
SOUTHEASTERN: Georgia
PACIFIC TEN: UCLA
IVY LEAGUE: Harvard,
   Dartmouth & Pennsylvania

1983 All-American Team
(O = Offense; D = Defense)
W R: Anthony Carter (Michigan)
T E: Gordon Hudson (Brigham Young)
L: Don Mosebar (O-USC), Steve Korte (O-Arkansas), Jimbo Covert (O-Pittsburgh), Bruce Matthews (O-USC), Billy Ray Smith (D- Arkansas), Vernon Maxwell (D-Arizona State), Mike Pitts (D-Alabama), Wilber Marshall (D-Florida), Gabriel Rivera (D-Texas Tech), Rick Bryan (D-Oklahoma), George Achica (D-USC)
C: Dave Rimington (Nebraska)
LB: Darryl Talley (West Virginia), Ricky Hunley (Arizona), Marcus Marek (Ohio State)
B: Terry Kinard (D-Clemson), Mike Richardson (D-Arizona State), Terry Hoage (D-Georgia), John Elway (QB-Stanford), Herschel Walker (RB-Georgia), Eric Dickerson (RB-Southern Methodist), Mike Rozier (RB-Nebraska)
K: Chuck Nelson (PK-Washington), Jim Arnold (P-Vanderbilt)

PROFESSIONAL REGULAR SEASON

The NFL Players Association calls a strike following the second week of the season. Play does not resume until Nov. 21. As a result, only 9 regular season games are played.

NFC
Eastern Division Winner: Washington (8-10-0). Quarterback Joe Theismann completes 64% of passes attempted to lead the NFC. Kicker Mark Moseley boots 20 out of 21 field goal tries.
Central Division Winner: Green Bay (5-3-1). The Packers make the playoffs for the first time since 1972. Quarterback Lynn Dickey leads the offense.
Western Division Winner: Atlanta (5-4-0). Running behind an All-Pro line, William Andrews and Gerald Riggs lead the Falcon offense.
League Leaders: *Passer:* Joe Theismann (Washington); *Rusher:* Tony Dorsett (Dallas); *Receiver:* Dwight Clark (San Francisco); *Scorer:* Wendell Tyler (L.A. Rams).

AFC
Eastern Division Winner: Miami (7-2-0). The Dolphins' pass defense and the running of fullback Andra Franklin are key factors as Miami repeats its division championship.
Central Division Winner: Cincinnati (7-2-0). Quarterback Ken Anderson sets an NFL season record with a 70.6% pass completion rate.
Western Division Winner: Los Angeles (8-1-0). Ted Hendricks heads the Raider defense in the team's first year in L.A. Halfback Marcus Allen and tight end Todd Christensen are also standouts.
League Leaders: *Passer:* Ken Anderson (Cincinnati); *Rusher:* Freeman McNeil (N.Y.); *Receiver:* Wes Chandler (San Diego); *Scorer:* Marcus Allen (L.A.).

Hall of Fame Inductees
Doug Atkins, Sam Huff, George Musso, Merlin Olsen

COLLEGE BOWLS & PRO CHAMPIONSHIPS

College Bowl Games
ROSE BOWL:
   UCLA 24, Michigan 14
SUGAR BOWL:
   Penn State 27, Georgia 23
COTTON BOWL:
   Southern Methodist 7,
   Pittsburgh 3
ORANGE BOWL:
   Nebraska 21, Louisiana State 17

NFC
Playoffs: The NFL tries a new playoff system, with "Wild Card" teams increased from 2 to 4. The system is dropped in the following year. First round: Washington 31, Detroit 7; Green Bay 41, St. Louis 10; Dallas 40, Tampa Bay 17; Minnesota 30, Atlanta 24. Second round: Washington 21, Minnesota 7; Dallas 37, Green Bay 26.
Championship Game: Washington 31, Dallas 17. Fullback John Riggins rushes for 140 yds behind the "Hogs" (offensive line) to lead the Redskins.

AFC
Playoffs: First round: Miami 28, New England 13; Los Angeles 27, Cleveland 10; New York 44, Cincinnati 17; San Diego 31, Pittsburgh 28. Second round: New York 17, Los Angeles 14; Miami 34, San Diego 13.
Championship Game: Miami 14, New York 0. A muddy field helps Miami win. After a scoreless 1st half, the Dolphins score on Woody Bennett's 7-yd run. Linebacker A.J. Duhe runs back an interception for 35 yds in the 4th quarter for the 2d Miami TD.

Super Bowl XVII
Washington 23, Miami 17. Miami takes a halftime lead, 17-10, but is held scoreless in the 2d half while the Redskins put 17 points on the board. Fullback John Riggins pounds out 166 yds (a Super Bowl record) as Washington wins its first championship since 1942. The Dolphin offense is held to less than 200 yds.

COLLEGE REGULAR SEASON

Nebraska, unbeaten and averaging 52 points per game, lays claim to being the greatest college football team ever assembled—until it is upset by once-beaten Miami, 31-30, in the Orange Bowl.

Mike Rozier, Nebraska's star running back, scores 29 TDs and averages 7.81 yds per carry, earning him the coveted Heisman Trophy.

Harvard beats Yale in the 100th game of this oldest college rivalry. Yale's record (1-9-0) is the worst in the school's 111 years of football.

Conference Champions:

BIG TEN: Illinois
BIG EIGHT: Nebraska
SOUTHWEST: Texas
SOUTHEASTERN: Auburn
PACIFIC TEN: UCLA
WESTERN ATHLETIC: BYU
ATLANTIC COAST: Maryland
IVY LEAGUE: Harvard & Pennsylvania

1983 All-American Team

(O = Offense; D = Defense)
WR: Irving Fryar (Nebraska)
TE: Gordon Hudson (Brigham Young)
L: Bill Fralic (O-Pittsburgh), Terry Long (O-East Carolina), Dean Steinkuhler (O-Nebraska), Doug Dawson (O-Texas), Rick Bryan (D-Oklahoma), Reggie White (D-Tennessee), William Perry (D- Clemson), William Fuller (D-North Carolina)
C: Tony Slaton (USC)
LB: Ricky Hunley (Arizona), Wilber Marshall (Florida), Ron Rivera (California), Jeff Leiding (Texas)
B: Russell Carter (Southern Methodist), Jerry Gray (D- Texas), Terry Hoage (D-Georgia), Don Rogers (D-UCLA), Steve Young (QB-Brigham Young), Mike Rozier (RB-Nebraska), Bo Jackson (RB-Auburn), Greg Allen (RB-Florida State), Napoleon McCallum (RB-Navy)
K: Luis Zendejas (PK-Arizona State), Jack Weil (P-Wyoming)

PROFESSIONAL REGULAR SEASON

NFC

Eastern Division Winner: Washington (14-2-0). Super Bowl champions repeat as division champs. Quarterback Joe Theismann throws 29 TD passes and gains 3,714 yds in the air. John Riggins rushes for 1,347 yds and 24 TDs.
Central Division Winner: Detroit (9-7-0). The Lions make the playoffs for the first time (last title came in 1957 when Detroit beat Cleveland for the NFL crown).
Western Division Winner: San Francisco (10-6-0). The 49ers regain the division title as quarterback Joe Montana returns to form (3,910 yds passing and 26 TDs). Receiver Dwight Clark snares 70 aerials.
League Leaders: *Passer:* Steve Bartkowski (Atlanta); *Rusher:* Eric Dickerson (L.A. Rams); *Receiver:* Roy Green (St. Louis); *Scorer:* John Riggins (Washington).

AFC

Eastern Division Winner: Miami (12-4-0). Rookie quarterback Dan Marino takes control, completing 175 passes (including 20 TDs).
Central Division Winner: Pittsburgh (10-6-0). Despite a season-long injury to star quarterback Terry Bradshaw, the Steelers win the division title. Fullback Franco Harris gains 1,007 yds rushing.
Western Division Winner: Los Angeles (12-4-0). After a poor start, quarterback Jim Plunkett tosses 20 TD passes and Marcus Allen rushes for 1,014 yds as the Rams retain the division title.
League Leaders: *Passer:* Dan Marino (Miami); *Rusher:* Curt Warner (Seattle); *Receiver:* Mark Duper (Miami); *Scorer:* Gary Anderson (Pittsburgh).

Hall of Fame Inductees

Bobby Bell, Sid Gillman, Sonny Jurgensen, Bobby Mitchell, Paul Warfield

COLLEGE BOWLS & PRO CHAMPIONSHIPS

College Bowl Games

ROSE BOWL:
  UCLA 45, Illinois 3
SUGAR BOWL:
  Auburn 9, Michigan 7
COTTON BOWL:
  Georgia 10, Texas 9
ORANGE BOWL:
  Miami 31, Nebraska 30

NFC

Playoffs: L.A. Rams 24, Dallas 17 (Wild Card); San Francisco 24, Detroit 23; Washington 51, L.A. Rams 7.
Championship Game: Washington 24, San Francisco 21. The Redskins hang on to repeat as NFC champions. Fullback John Riggins rushes for 123 yds and 2 TDs. Mark Moseley's 4th quarter field goal with 40 seconds left wins for Washington after 49er quarterback Joe Montana hurls 3 TD passes in the 4th quarter to even the score.

AFC

Playoffs: Seattle 31, Denver 7 (Wild Card); Seattle 27, Miami 20; L.A. Raiders 38, Pittsburgh 10.
Championship Game: Los Angeles 31, Seattle 14. The Raiders build a 20-0 halftime lead and coast to their first AFC championship (in L.A.). Quarterback Jim Plunkett passes for 214 yds and Marcus Allen rushes for 154 yds to lead the Raiders. Seahawk star Curt Warner is held to 26 yds rushing on 11 carries.

Super Bowl XVII

Los Angeles 38, Washington 9. The Raiders move ahead, 21-3, at the half and are never in trouble. Halfback Marcus Allen rushes for 191 yds in 20 carries, including a 74-yd dash in the 3d quarter. Washington's star runner John Riggins is held to 64 yds in 26 carries.

COLLEGE REGULAR SEASON

Brigham Young (13-0), unbeaten in 24 straight games, wins the national championship to become the fifth team in a row to earn that distinction for the first time.

Quarterback Doug Flutie of Boston College, the nation's leading passer, ends his career dramatically, hurling the ball 64 yds for a TD on the last play for an upset victory over Miami. Flutie also wins the Heisman Trophy.

Conference Champions
BIG TEN: Ohio State
BIG EIGHT: Oklahoma
PACIFIC TEN: USC
SOUTHEASTERN: Florida
SOUTHWEST: Houston
WESTERN ATHLETIC: BYU
ATLANTIC COAST: Maryland
IVY LEAGUE: Pennsylvania

1984 All-American Team
(O = Offense; D = Defense)
WR: David Williams (Illinois), Eddie Brown (Miami, Fla.)
TE: Jay Novacek (Wyoming)
L: Bill Fralic (O-Pittsburgh), Lomas Brown (O-Florida), Del Wilkes (O-South Carolina), Jim Lachey (O-Ohio State), Bill Mayo (O-Tennessee), Bruce Smith (D-Virginia Tech), Tony Degrate (D-Texas), Ron Holmes (D-Washington), Tony Casillas (D-Oklahoma)
C: Mark Traynowicz (Nebraska)
LB: Gregg Carr (Auburn), Jack Del Rio (USC), Larry Station (Iowa)
B: Jerry Gray (D-Texas), Tony Thurman (D-Boston College), Jeff Sanchez (D-Georgia), David Fulcher (D-Arizona State), Rod Brown (D-Oklahoma State), Doug Flutie (QB-Boston College), Keith Byars (RB- Ohio State), Kenneth Davis (RB-Texas Christian), Reuben Mayes (RB-Washington State).
K: Kevin Butler (PK-Georgia), Ricky Anderson (P-Vanderbilt)

PROFESSIONAL REGULAR SEASON

NFC
Eastern Division Winner: Washington (11-5-0). Redskins win their third straight NFC East title. Quarterback Joe Theismann tosses 24 TD passes and gains 3,391 yds.
Central Division Winner: Chicago (10-6-0). The Bears' Walter Payton gains 1,654 yds and breaks Jim Brown's career rushing record.
Western Division Winner: San Francisco (15-1-0). Quarterback Joe Montana tosses 28 TD passes and gains 3,630 yds in the air. Wendell Tyler and Roger Craig rush for 1,911 yds.
League Leaders: *Passer:* Neil Lomax (St. Louis); *Rusher:* Eric Dickerson (Los Angeles). Dickerson breaks O.J. Simpson's single season rushing mark with 2,007 yds; *Receiver:* Roy Green (St. Louis); *Scorer:* Ray Wersching (San Francisco).

AFC
Eastern Division Winner: Miami (14-2-0). The Dolphins capture their 4th division title in a row. Quarterback Dan Marino sets new NFL records with 48 TD passes and 5,084 yds in the air.
Central Division Winner: Pittsburgh (9-7-0). Quarterback Terry Bradshaw retires and veteran fullback Franco Harris is cut, but the Steelers still retain their title in a weak division.
Western Division Winner: Denver (13-3-0). John Elway takes over at quarterback and leads the Broncos to their first division title since 1978.
League Leaders: *Passer:* Ken Anderson (Cincinnati); *Rusher:* Earnest Jackson (San Diego); *Receiver:* Mark Clayton (Miami); *Scorer:* Gary Anderson (Pittsburgh).

Hall of Fame Inductees
Willie Brown, Mike McCormack, Charley Taylor, Arnie Weinmeister

COLLEGE BOWLS & PRO CHAMPIONSHIPS

College Bowl Games
ROSE BOWL:
USC 20, Ohio State 17
SUGAR BOWL:
Nebraska 28, LSU 10
COTTON BOWL:
Boston College 45, Houston 28
ORANGE BOWL:
Washington 28, Oklahoma 17

NFC
Playoffs: N.Y. 16, L.A. 13 (Wild Card); San Francisco 21, N.Y. 10; Chicago 23, Washington 19.
Championship Game: San Francisco 23, Chicago 0. 49er quarterback Joe Montana gains 233 yds in the air and Ray Wersching boots 3 field goals. San Francisco's defense sacks Bear quarterback Steve Fuller 9 times and holds Walter Payton under 100 yds rushing.

AFC
Playoffs: Seattle 13, L.A. Raiders 7 (Wild Card); Miami 31, Seattle 10; Pittsburgh 24, Denver 17.
Championship Game: Miami 45, Pittsburgh 28. Dolphin quarterback Dan Marino completes 21 out of 32 attempts for 421 yds and 4 TDs in a high-scoring game. The Miami defense picks off 3 Steeler passes and recovers a key fumble.

Super Bowl XIX
San Francisco 38, Miami 16. In a clash between superstar quarterbacks, Joe Montana outperforms Dan Marino, tossing 3 TD passes and scoring TD #4 on a 6-yd run. Miami is held scoreless in the 2d half as the 49er defense limits the Dolphins to 25 yds on the ground.

COLLEGE REGULAR SEASON

Oklahoma (11-1-0) wins its 6th national championship following its defeat of top-ranked Penn State, 25-10, in the Orange Bowl.

Halfback Bo Jackson of Auburn takes the Heisman Trophy, finishing ahead of Chuck Long (Iowa) by the closest margin in the award's history.

Joe Dudek of Plymouth State sets all-time career records with 79 TDs and 474 points scored.

Conference Champions
BIG TEN: Iowa
BIG EIGHT: Oklahoma
SOUTHEASTERN: Tennessee
ATLANTIC COAST: Maryland
WESTERN ATHLETIC: Brigham Young & Air Force
SOUTHWEST: Texas A&M
PACIFIC TEN: UCLA
IVY LEAGUE: Pennsylvania

1985 All-American Team
(O = Offense; D = Defense)
WR: David Williams (Illinois), Tim McGee (Tennessee)
TE: Willie Smith (Miami, Fla.)
L: Jim Dombrowski (O-Virginia), Jeff Bregel (O-USC), Brian Jozwiak (O-West Virginia), John Rienstra (O-Temple), J.D. Maarleveld (O-Maryland), Jamie Dukes (O-Florida State), Tim Green (D-Syracuse), Leslie O'Neal (D-Oklahoma State), Tony Casillas (D-Oklahoma), Mike Ruth (D-Boston College), Mike Hammerstein (D-Michigan)
C: Pete Anderson (Georgia)
LB: Brian Bosworth (Oklahoma), Larry Station (Iowa), Johnny Holland (Texas A&M)
B: David Fulcher (D-Arizona State), Brad Cochran (D-Michigan), Scott Thomas (D-Air Force), Chuck Long (QB-Iowa), Bo Jackson (RB-Auburn), Lorenzo White (RB-Michigan State), Thurman Thomas (RB-Oklahoma State), Reggie Dupard (RB-Southern Methodist), Napoleon McCallum (RB-Navy)
K: John Lee (PK-UCLA), Barry Helton (P-Colorado)

PROFESSIONAL REGULAR SEASON

NFC
Eastern Division Winner: Dallas (10-6-0). The aging Cowboys regain the NFC East title after a 4-year drought. Quarterback Danny White throws 21 TD passes and Tony Dorsett runs for 1,307 yds.
Central Division Winner: Chicago (15-1-0). The Bears' only loss is to Miami. Walter Payton adds 1,551 yds to his all-time rushing record.
Western Division Winner: Los Angeles (11-5-0). The Rams beat the 49ers in a showdown game against the Super Bowl champs to win the title. Fullback Eric Dickerson scores 12 TDs and rushes 1,234 yds.
League Leaders: *Passer:* Joe Montana (San Francisco); *Rusher:* Gerald Riggs (Atlanta); *Receiver:* Mike Quick (Philadelphia); *Scorer:* Kevin Butler (Chicago).

AFC
Eastern Division Winner: Miami (12-4-0). The Dolphins win their last 7 games in a row as quarterback Dan Marino throws 30 TD passes and gains 4,137 yds in the air to lead the offense.
Central Division Winner: Cleveland (8-8-0). The Browns take the title despite a .500 season. Halfback Kevin Mack and fullback Earnest Byner both rush over 1,000 yds.
Western Division Winner: Los Angeles (12-4-0). All-Pro halfback Marcus Allen rushes for 1,759 yds, scores 14 TDs and catches 67 passes. Cornerback Mike Haynes leads the best defense in the AFC.
League Leaders: *Passer:* Ken O'Brien (N.Y.); *Rusher:* Marcus Allen (L.A. Raiders); *Receiver:* Steve Largent (Seattle); *Scorer:* Gary Anderson (Pittsburgh).

Hall of Fame Inductees
Frank Gatski, Joe Namath, Pete Rozelle, O.J. Simpson, Roger Staubach

COLLEGE BOWLS & PRO CHAMPIONSHIPS

College Bowl Games
ROSE BOWL:
   UCLA 45, Iowa 28
SUGAR BOWL:
   Tennessee 35, Miami 7
COTTON BOWL:
   Texas A&M 36, Auburn 16
ORANGE BOWL:
   Oklahoma 25, Penn State 10

NFC
Playoffs: N.Y. 17, San Francisco 3 (Wild Card); Los Angeles Rams 20, Dallas 0; Chicago 21, N.Y. 0.
Championship Game: Chicago 24, L.A. Rams 0. The Bears jump out in front on quarterback Jim McMahon's 16-yd run and are never threatened. Chicago adds TDs in the 3d and 4th quarters (including Wilber Marshall's 52-yd runback of a fumble recovery), while its defense shuts down the Ram offense (130 net yds).

AFC
Playoffs: New England 26, N.Y. 14 (Wild Card); Miami 24, Cleveland 21; New England 27, L.A. Raiders 20.
Championship Game: New England 31, Miami 14. The "Wild Card" Patriots upset Miami with their running game (255 yds), 4 fumble recoveries and 2 interceptions of Dan Marino passes. New England quarterback Tony Eason throws 3 short TD passes.

Super Bowl XX
Chicago 46, New England 10. New England scores first, but the Bears quickly recover and lead 23-3 at the half. A 21-point 3d quarter produces the most one-sided game in Super Bowl history. The Chicago defense recovers 4 Patriot fumbles, intercepts 2 Steve Grogan passes, and allows an amazingly low 7 yds rushing total.

COLLEGE REGULAR SEASON

Penn State wins its 2d national championship in 5 years, defeating #2 Miami (Fla.) 14-10 in the Fiesta Bowl. Coach Joe Paterno ties Paul ("Bear") Bryant of Alabama for the most undefeated regular seasons (6).

Miami quarterback Vinny Testaverde (26 TD passes) wins the Heisman Trophy. Paul Palmer of Temple sets a new single season record of 2,633 all-purpose yds.

Conference Champions
BIG TEN: Michigan
BIG EIGHT: Oklahoma
PACIFIC TEN: Arizona State
SOUTHEASTERN: Louisiana State
SOUTHWEST: Texas A&M
ATLANTIC COAST: Clemson
WESTERN ATHLETIC: San Diego State
IVY LEAGUE: Pennsylvania

1986 All-American Team
(O = Offense; D = Defense)
WR: Cris Carter (Ohio State)
TE: Keith Jackson (Oklahoma)
L: Jeff Bregel (O-USC), Randy Dixon (O-Pittsburgh), Danny Villa (O-Arizona State), John Clay (O-Missouri), Jerome Brown (D- Miami, Fla.), Danny Noonan (D-Nebraska), Tony Woods (D-Pittsburgh), Jason Buck (D-Brigham Young), Reggie Rogers (D-Washington)
C: Ben Tamburello (Auburn)
LB: Cornelius Bennett (Alabama), Shane Conlan (Penn State), Brian Bosworth (Oklahoma), Chris Spielman (Ohio State)
B: Thomas Everett (D-Baylor), Tim McDonald (D-USC), Bennie Blades (D-Miami, Fla.), Rod Woodson (D-Purdue), Garland Rivers (D-Michigan), Vinnie Testaverde (QB-Miami, Fla.), Brent Fullwood (RB-Auburn), Paul Palmer (RB-Temple), Terrence Flagler (RB-Clemson), Brad Muster (RB-Stanford), D.J. Dozier (RB-Penn State)
K: Barry Helton (P-Colorado), Jeff Jaeger (PK-Washington)

PROFESSIONAL REGULAR SEASON

NFC
Eastern Division Winner: New York (14-2-0). Quarterback Phil Simms throws 21 TD passes and gains 3,487 yds in the air. Running back Joe Morris rushes for 1,516 yds and linebacker Lawrence Taylor leads the NFL in sacks.
Central Division Winner: Chicago (14-2-0). Despite losing quarterback Jim McMahon for the season with a shoulder injury, the Bears drop only 2 contests. Walter Payton rushes for 1,333 yds and 8 TDs. The defense allows only 187 points.
Western Division Winner: San Francisco (10-5-1). Quarterback Joe Montana leads the 49ers to a division title. Free safety Ronnie Lott picks off 10 interceptions.
League Leaders: *Passer:* Tommy Kramer (Minnesota); *Rusher:* Eric Dickerson (Los Angeles); *Receiver:* Jerry Rice (San Francisco); *Scorer:* Kevin Butler (Chicago).

AFC
Eastern Division Winner: New England (11-5-0). Quarterbacks Tony Eason and Steve Grogan combine for 27 TD passes and 4,300 passing yds
Central Division Winner: Cleveland (12-4-0). Quarterback Bernie Kosar in his second year leads the Browns to the title with 310 completions for 3,854 yds and 17 TDs.
Western Division Winner: Denver (11-5-0). Quarterback John Elway scrambles for 257 yds and passes for 3,485 yds and 19 TDs.
League Leaders: *Passer:* Dan Marino (Miami); *Rusher:* Curt Warner (Seattle); *Receiver:* Stanley Morgan (New England); *Scorer:* Tony Franklin (New England).

Hall of Fame Inductees
Paul Hornung, Ken Houston, Willie Lanier, Fran Tarkenton, Doak Walker

COLLEGE BOWLS & PRO CHAMPIONSHIPS

College Bowl Games
ROSE BOWL:
Arizona State 22, Michigan 15
SUGAR BOWL:
Nebraska 30, Louisiana State 15
COTTON BOWL:
Ohio State 28, Texas A&M 12
ORANGE BOWL:
Oklahoma 42, Arkansas 8
FIESTA BOWL:
Penn State 14, Miami 10

NFC
Playoffs: Washington 19, Los Angeles 7 (Wild Card); Washington 27, Chicago 13; New York 49, San Francisco 3.
Championship Game: New York Giants 17, Washington 0. The Giants take a 17-0 lead at halftime. Both teams are held scoreless in the 2d half. New York's running game produces 117 yds and its defense holds the Redskins to 40 yds on the ground.

AFC
Playoffs: New York 35, Kansas City 15 (Wild Card); Cleveland 20, New York 17 (2 OTs); Denver 22, New England 17.
Championship Game: Denver 23, Cleveland 20. Quarterbacks Bernie Kosar (Cleveland) and John Elway (Denver) lead their teams to a 20-20 tie at the end of regulation time. Rich Karlis boots the winning field goal in overtime to win for Denver. A fumble and 2 interceptions prove costly for the Browns.

Super Bowl XXI
New York 39, Denver 20. Behind 10-9 at the half, the Giants explode for 30 points in the 2d half to win decisively. Denver quarterback John Elway passes for 304 yds, but the Giant defense holds the Bronco ground game to 52 yds. New York quarterback Phil Simms completes 22 of 25 passes to set a Super Bowl record (88% completion rate).

1987

COLLEGE REGULAR SEASON

Miami (Fla.) captures the #1 ranking by beating Oklahoma in the Orange Bowl. Florida State, whose only loss is to Miami, is ranked #2, making this the first time since the AP polls began in 1934 that the top two teams are from the same state.

Columbia finishes the season with its 40th straight loss to extend the longest losing streak in major college football history.

Flanker Tim Brown of Notre Dame is only the 3d non-back to win the Heisman Trophy.

Conference Champions
BIG TEN: Michigan State
BIG EIGHT: Oklahoma
SOUTHEASTERN: Auburn
PACIFIC TEN: USC
SOUTHWEST: Texas A&M
WESTERN ATHLETIC: Wyoming
IVY LEAGUE: Harvard

1987 All-American Team
(O = Offense; D = Defense)
WR: Tim Brown (Notre Dame), Wendell Davis (Louisiana State)
TE: Keith Jackosn (O-Oklahoma)
L: Mark Hutson (O-Oklahoma State), Dave Cadigan (O-USC), John Elliott (O-Michigan), Randall McDaniel (O-Arizona State), Daniel Stubbs (D-Miami, Fla.), Chad Hennings (D-Air Force), Tracy Rocker (D-Auburn), Ted Gregory (D-Syracuse), John Roper (D-Texas A&M)
C: Nacho Albergamo (Louisiana State)
LB: Chris Spielman (Ohio State), Audray Bruce (Auburn), Dante Jones (Oklahoma)
B: Bennie Blades (D-Miami, Fla.), Deion Sanders (D-Florida State), Rickey Dixon (D-Oklahoma), Chuck Cecil (D-Arizona), Don McPherson (QB-Syracuse), Lorenzo White (RB-Michigan State), Craig Heyward (RB-Pittsburgh)
K: David Treadwell (PK-Ohio State), Tom Tupa (P-Ohio State)

PROFESSIONAL REGULAR SEASON

NFC
Eastern Division Winner: Washington (11-4). The Redskins lead the rest of their division by 4 games behind the passing and scrambling of quarterback Doug Williams.
Central Division Winner: Chicago (11-4). The Bears win their 4th straight division title. Superstar Walter Payton retires after 13 years with 16,726 rushing yds among several all-time career records.
Western Division Winner: San Francisco (13-2). The 49ers, led by quarterback Joe Montana, lead the NFL in scoring (30.6 points per game) and offense (399 yards per game).
Conference Leaders: *Passer:* Joe Montana (San Francisco); *Rusher:* Charles White (Los Angeles Rams); *Receiver:* J.T. Smith (St. Louis); *Scorer:* Jerry Rice (San Francisco).

AFC
Eastern Division Winner: Indianapolis (9-6). The Colts edge out Miami by one game as its newly acquired superstar, Eric Dickerson, scrambles for 1,288 yds.
Central Division Winner: Cleveland (10-5). The Browns take the title by one game over Houston. A tough defense and timely scoring keep them on top.
Western Division Winner: Denver (10-4-1). The Broncos are led by quarterback John Elway's passing and a tough defense.
Conference Leaders: *Passer:* John Elway (Denver); *Rusher:* Bo Jackson (Los Angeles Raiders); *Receiver:* Al Toon (New York); *Scorer:* Jim Breech (Cincinnati).

Hall of Fame Inductees
Larry Csonka, Len Dawson, Joe Green, John Henry Johnson, Jim Langer, Don Maynard, Gene Upshaw

COLLEGE BOWLS & PRO CHAMPIONSHIPS

College Bowl Games
ROSE BOWL:
  Michigan State 20, USC 17
SUGAR BOWL:
  Syracuse 16, Auburn 16. This is the first tie game in Sugar Bowl history.
COTTON BOWL:
  Texas A&M 35, Notre Dame 10
ORANGE BOWL:
  Miami 20, Oklahoma 14
FIESTA BOWL:
  Florida State 31, Nebraska 28

NFC
Playoffs: Minnesota 44, New Orleans 10 (Wild Card); Washington 21, Chicago 17; Minnesota 36, San Francisco 24.
Championship Game: Washington 17, Minnesota 10. The Redskins' defense stars with 8 sacks and 2 goal line stands in the 4th quarter.

AFC
Playoffs: Houston 23, Seattle 20 (Wild Card game in overtime); Denver 34, Houston 10; Cleveland 38, Indianapolis 21.
Championship Game: Denver 38, Cleveland 33. Quarterback John Elway connects for 281 yards and 3 TD passes to lead the Broncos.

Super Bowl XXII
Washington 42, Denver 10. The Redskins, after spotting Denver 10 points in the opening period, storm back with a record-setting 35 points in the 2d quarter as Denver suffers its 2d straight Super Bowl defeat. Washington quarterback Doug Williams passes for 340 yds and Tim Smith rushes for another 204, both Super Bowl records. Ricky Sanders scores 2 TDs and gains 193 yds on pass receptions, including an 80-yd completion from Williams. Denver's John Elway completes 14 passes for 257 yds, but 3 interceptions and a weak running attack prove costly.

COLLEGE REGULAR SEASON

Barry Sanders, Oklahoma State's premiere junior running back, is awarded the Heisman Trophy after breaking Marcus Allen's career rushing mark (2,342 yds).

Notre Dame's dramatic 31-30 defeat of Miami (Fla.) is the best game of the season. Instead of settling for a tie, the Hurricanes opt for the two-point conversion and fail, costing Miami the national championship.

Conference Champions

BIG TEN: Michigan
BIG EIGHT: Nebraska
PACIFIC 10: USC
SOUTHESTERN: Aurburn & LSU
SOUTHWEST: Arkansas
IVY LEAGUE: Cornell & Penn

1988 All-American Team

(O = Offense; D = Deffense)
WR: Hart Lee Dykes (Oklahoma State), Jason Phillips (Houston).
TE: Wesley Watts (Mississippi).
E: Frank Stams (D-Notre Dame), Broderick Thomas (D-Nebraska).
T: Andy Heck (O-Notre Dame), Tony Mandarich (O-Michigan State).
G: Anthony Phillips (O-Oklahoma), Mike Utley (O-Washington State).
C: Jake Young (O-Nebraska).
L: Wayne Martin (D-Arkansas), Mark Messner (D-Michigan), Tracy Rocker (Auburn).
LB: Keith DeLong (Tennessee), Mike Stonebreaker (Notre Dame), Derrick Thomas (Alabama).
B: Darren Lewis (O-Texas A&M), Barry Sanders (O-Oklahoma State), Louis Oliver (D-Florida), Markus Paul (D-Syracuse), Deion Sanders (D-Florida State).
QB: Steve Walsh (Miami).
K: Kendall Trainor (PK-Arkansas), Keith English (P-Colorado).

PROFESSIONAL REGULAR SEASON

NFC

Eastern Division Winner: Philadelphia (10-6). Quarterback Randall Cunningham and a tenacious defensive secondary power the Eagles to their first division title since 1980.
Central Division Winner: Chicago (12-4). The Bears' vaunted defense carries a weak offense (its first year without Walter Payton) for the team's 5th straight division title.
Western Division Winner: San Francisco (10-6). The 49ers, paced by quarterback Joe Montana, running back Roger Craig, and wide receiver Jerry Rice, win their 5th division title in the 1980s.
League Leaders: *Passer:* Wade Wilson (Minnesota); *Rusher:* Herschel Walker (Dallas); *Receiver:* Henry Ellard (Los Angeles); *Scorer:* Jim Cofer (San Francisco).

AFC

Eastern Division Winner: Buffalo (12-4). Jim Kelly's passing attack and a stingy defense pace the Bills to their first division title since 1980.
Central Division Winner: Cincinnati (12-4). The Bengals defeat the Super Bowl XXII champion Washington Redskins in their final game to clinch their first division title in 7 years.
Western Division Winner: Seattle (9-7). The Seahawks win the first division title in their 13-year history behind quaterback Dave Krieg.
League Leaders: *Passer:* Boomer Esiason (Cincinnati); *Rusher:* Eric Dickerson (Indianapolis); *Receiver:* Al Toon (New York); *Scorer:* Scott Norwood (Buffalo).

COLLEGE BOWLS & PRO CHAMPIONSHIPS

ROSE BOWL:
   Michigan 22, USC 14
COTTON BOWL:
   UCLA 17, Arkansas 3
ORANGE BOWL:
   Miami (Fla.) 27, Nebraska 3
SUGAR BOWL:
   Florida State 13, Auburn 7
FIESTA BOWL:
   Notre Dame 34, West Virginia 21. Notre Dame finishes the season with a perfect record (12-0) and is the unanimous choice for #1 in the nation. This is the school's 8th undefeated season, the most for any U.S. college in history.

NFC

Playoffs: Minnesota 20, Los Angeles Rams 17 (Wild Card); Chicago 20, Philadelphia 12; San Francisco 34, Minnesota 9.
Championship Game: San Francisco 28, Chicago 3. San Francisco quarterback Joe Montana completes 17 out of 27 to lead the 49ers. Wide receiver Jerry Rice catches 5 passes for 123 yds and 2 TDs.

AFC

Playoffs: Houston 24, Cleveland 23 (Wild Card); Buffalo 17, Houston 0; Cincinnati 21, Seattle 13.
Championship Game: Cincinnati 21, Buffalo 10. Rookie sensation Ickey Woods gains 102 yds in 29 carries, including 2 TDs. Jim Kelly, Buffalo's star quarterback, suffers 3 interceptions.

Super Bowl XXIII

San Francisco 20, Cincinnati 16. Joe Montana and Jerry Rice put on a spectacular show in the waning seconds to lead San Francisco to victory over the Bengals in what most observers feel is the most dramatic and exciting Super Bowl game ever played. Rice snares 11 passes to tie one Super Bowl record and gains 215 yds to break another. Montana completes 23 out of 36 attempts for 357 yds, a Super Bowl record.

While only a rookie, quarterback **Dan Marino** leads the Miami Dolphins into the NFL playoffs. Malcom W. Emmons

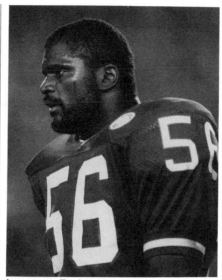

Lawrence Taylor of the New York Giants, considered by many to be the greatest linebacker in the history of professional football. Malcom W. Emmons

Tony Dorsett of the Dallas Cowboys ducks a tackler and heads upfield. Malcom W. Emmons

Coach **Paul Brown,** a head coach in the NFL for more than 40 years, gives instructions to his Cincinnati Bengal quarterback. Malcom W. Emmons

Former Notre Dame quarterback **Joe Montana** quickly establishes himself in the NFL, leading the San Francisco 49ers to their first Super Bowl win. Malcom W. Emmons

Coach **Bear Bryant**, the "winningest" coach in college football history, with 323 victories recorded in 38 years. Malcom W. Emmons

BIBLIOGRAPHY

Americana Encyclopedia Yearbooks (1923-1987).

Carruth, Gorton and Ehrlich, Eugene. *Facts & Dates of American Sports*. New York: Harper & Row/Perennial Library, 1988.

Danzig, Allison. *Oh, How They Played the Game*. New York: Macmillan, 1971.

Davis, Mac. *Strange & Incredible Sports Happenings*. New York: Grosset & Dunlap, 1982.

Encyclopaedia Britannica Yearbooks, 1923-1987.

McCallum, John. *Ivy League Football Since 1872*. New York: Stein & Day, 1977.

NCAA Football Record Book 1988. Mission, Ks.: National Collegiate Athletic Association, 1988.

Neft, David and Cohen, Richard M., eds. *The Sports Encyclopedia: Pro Football, The Modern Era* (1960 to 1987), 5th ed. New York: St. Martins Press/Sports Products Inc., 1987.

New York Times (Sports Sections, 1920-1988). New York: New York Times Co.

Sporting News Football Trivia Book, The. St. Louis, Mo.: Sporting News Pub. Co., 1985.

Wright, Graeme, ed. *Rand McNally Illustrated Dictionary of Sports*. Chicago: Rand McNally Pub. Co., 1978.

INDEX